My name is Marie and I'm a workaholic. I have spent years throwing everything I had into my career, chasing that next promotion, never satisfied. My goal was always to become a chief marketing officer, when I achieved that was, I satisfied—nope! Which is exactly why every word on every page of this book resonated so deeply with me, as if it was written for me. My inability to balance my career aspirations with life almost cost me my marriage, and certainly has cost me precious time with my family. Enough is enough, and this book has shined a bright, shining light on the path I need to take to change my life, without giving up my career goals. My only critique, I wish I'd found it sooner!　　**—Marie Still,** Executive Vice President/GM & Author

I started working at the age of sixteen. I always thought if I worked hard enough someday it would pay off. Days turned to years and years to decades. I finally learned that working all the time without any balance destroys relationships, health, and happiness. It was many hard lessons to learn over many years that are years now lost! **Kick Ass and Have a Life** provides clear and effective steps to change the destructive behavior of workaholism and avoid the loss of so many years of life. I am finding time that I never knew existed. Now I know it was there all the time I just didn't have the tools to balance my career and my life. This book is a must-read!
　　—Donald McCormack, Systems Engineer/Entrepreneur

I was a workaholic for 20 years. It was my goal to become an operations manager and a designer. I know, two very different careers and I managed to become both an operations manager and a design manager. At the expense of my mental health and if I hadn't had such an understanding and supportive husband, I probably would have lost my marriage also. This book has been my savior. Along with Paula Marie's anecdotes, which ran very close to home. The toolboxes are invaluable, and my life has turned around. I now make time for myself, and my husband and we vacation regularly. Thank You Paula Marie!!

—Lucinda Lewis, Operations Manager/ Designer

I was a workaholic until chronic pain and fatigue brought my career to a sudden halt. I wish this book would have been available twenty-five years ago. I know this is going to help so many people to live a more balanced life, and still have a thriving career! I have made some big changes in my life over the last several years, and I look forward to making more positive changes and dreaming bigger, while staying balanced, using the tools in **Kick Ass and Have a Life!** The toolboxes are simple, and Paula Marie has created easy ways to implement them into everyday living. I really love it! It is easy to read, entertaining, and inspiring! Really great work!   **—Stacey Townsend,** Chronic Pain Coach

Thank goodness I found Paula's wonderful book! Her eight-toolbox system for time management helped me to restructure my life and recapture the joy and enthusiasm I used to feel every day. Paula—you're a miracle worker!   **—Barb Wilson,** CEO/Edit Partner

Unlock the Secrets
to Extraordinary Living

KICK ASS

AND

HAVE A LIFE

8 POWERFUL TOOLS
to Manage Your Time & Transform Your Life

PAULA MARIE

Unlock the Secrets to Extraordinary Living
Kick Ass and Have a Life!
8 Powerful tools to Manage Your Time & Transform Your Life
Copyright © 2022 Paula Marie
All rights reserved.

Published by Elife Living LLC

The author is not a health care expert, counselor, or expert. The reader should consult a physician and or counselor in matters relating to their mental, financial or physical health, particularly regarding any symptoms that may require diagnosis or medical attention. This book is not intended as a substitute for the medical advice of physicians or financial experts. Readers of this book release the author from any liability related to its contents.

The author has tried to recreate events, locales, and conversations from memories. To protect privacy, in some instances, the author changed the names of individuals and places and some identifying characteristics and details such as physical properties, occupations, and places of residence.

Although the author has made every effort to ensure that the information in this book was correct at press time, the author does not assume and hereby disclaims any liability to any party for any loss, damage, or disruption caused by errors or omissions, whether such errors or omissions result from negligence, accident, or any other cause.

This book was published under the pseudonym (pen name) Paula Marie. It should be noted, however, that the book's events took place under the author's legal name.

Library of Congress Control Number: 2022901746
ISBN paperback: 978-1-7360464-6-3
ISBN hardcover: 978-1-7360464-8-7
ISBN eBook: 978-1-7360464-7-0

First Printing, First Edition 2023
Printed in the United States of America

10 9 8 7 6 5 4 3 2 1

To Brooke,

You are and always will be my "Why"

You have taught me so much,

including the life lessons contained in these pages.

May you never lose sight of the value of time.

~ Paula Marie

All we have to decide
is what to do with the time
that is given us.

~J.R.R TOLKIEN

Contents

Introduction

Why did I write this book? There are already thousands of self-help books on the market. Well, quite simply, I have a story to share that can change your life. Now, I know that is quite a claim. I don't know you or anything about your life, so how in the world can I hope to change it?

Here's the thing: I have a feeling my story may not be that different from yours. After all, you took the time to pick up this book. You may share my same experiences, and you may be on the same track I was on before I learned how to kick ass and have a life.

All of us have a past, and that past makes us who we are today. I lost fifteen years of my life to workaholism. Those years are gone, wasted, and I can't get them back. But the life lessons that I learned the hard way enabled me to escape the fog of that lifestyle. I'm sharing them on these pages because they can help other workaholics, too. If only I had known the things I know now during those years, I could have drastically changed my course. So, if I help just one person avoid suffering the loss that I suffered, this book will have served its purpose.

Who am I, and what makes me qualified to write this book?

Well, maybe it would be easier to tell you who I'm *not*.

I'm not a therapist or a psychologist; I'm not a brilliant scholar or someone who pretends to know it all. I'm a hard-working, highly motivated woman who spent most of my life focusing on just one thing—success—only to watch my world fall apart when I finally attained it.

Disillusioned by my former belief that money and success would bring happiness, I had to start over. I rose from the darkness and let go of the "lost days" that I can never get back.

How did I do it?

I created a system that enabled me both to kick ass and to have a life!

And what does my life look like today? To start, I'm free to have great experiences, enjoy the things I worked so hard for,

Introduction **3**

and be present in the moment. I live in my dream home, am married to the love of my life (after getting it really wrong the first time), have financial security (which I chased for years), and sometimes have to pinch myself when I glance around the life I have created. The journey was long, and I wasted many years living as a workaholic.

My hope is that my story and the eight toolboxes I created will enrich your life, saving you precious time. These toolboxes provide specific tools to manage and overcome your workaholic habits and drastically improve your lifestyle.

What if I told you the life you've always dreamed of doesn't require you to work so hard? You can have time for your family, friends, health, and hobbies and still be successful behind your wildest dreams.

Would you believe me?

That is exactly what I'm about to prove to you in this book.

You're probably wondering what it takes to transform yourself from a person drowning in work and stuck in the grip of a workaholic addiction to one who is successful in a career and having an amazing life. After all, it sounds far-fetched, right?

Well, this is where you decide to stick around and find out if there is anything to these tall claims, or you can scan a few pages and jump back on your laptop. This is one of those defining moments when you will make a decision that could change your life.

Stick with me, and let's explore the concept of rejecting the workaholic existence and creating the life you actually want.

Not the one you think you should have or the one you somehow got stuck with along the way.

The life you deserve.

The life you'll love, the life that you desire!

Read on…

1
The Beginning

With my chin tucked to my chest, I stepped into the dimly lit room. My gaze flitted around the room, avoiding eye contact with the surprising amount of people filling it. I spotted a chair and quickly made my way through the crowd before collapsing into it, hoping to avoid unnecessary attention. Everyone was speaking in hushed whispers. The people were from all ages and walks of life, and each one of them had their own story—but we were all there for the same reason.

We were there to take an exam we hoped would change our lives.

The clock started. I tried to focus on the questions displayed on the monitor in front of me, but the rhythmic ticking of the timer in the bottom right corner of the screen dominated my thoughts. Twelve minutes passed as I read the first few questions over and over.

Breaking out in a cold sweat, I realized I didn't know the answers.

I had walked into that room hopeful and proud. Sure, I had studied harder than anyone else—endless hours, sleepless nights; I had spent the last four months studying daily. To most, it was simply a real estate exam.

But to me, it was so much more.

It was my chance to live the life I'd dreamed of, to gain financial freedom, to be truly successful. For me, in that moment, it was—*everything*.

I tried to calm my racing thoughts, but my anxiety was rising, and with each passing second, the panic grew as my confidence plummeted. I forced myself to answer a few questions, sure I was getting them wrong. It was as if the endless facts on contracts and deeds and Fair Housing Laws, and so much more had vanished from my brain the second that monotonous ticking timer started.

We were given four hours to complete the exam. When the clock ran out, the computer would shut off, and the test would be graded on the spot. Scoring seventy-five percent or higher was required to pass. If you passed, you'd be eligible to apply for your real estate license. If you failed, you'd get your score, and you could schedule a retake. A retake was simply not an option. I put in the work. I *had* to pass—my future was waiting.

Two hours into the exam, I was still nervous and unsure, but I was feeling a little better. The confidence I'd earned was slowly returning. Suddenly, the sound of a chair scraping back caught my attention. The man next to me stood and left.

How can he be finished?

About thirty minutes later, a choir of scraping chairs and departing footsteps signaled several more people completing their exam and leaving. I sat alone in a mostly deserted room. I wasn't even halfway finished. Praying for guidance, I tried to focus.

One hour later, I was the only one left in the room. Insecurity raged through my soul. *Who am I kidding? I can't do this.* Old insecurities mixed with new ones; after all, tests had never been my strong point. I took a deep breath and pressed on.

With fifteen minutes remaining, I had miraculously answered every question. I reread questions, changed a few answers, working until the very last second. The timer ticked to zero, and the screen went dark.

I closed my eyes and said one more prayer, then picked up my pen and walked out of the room.

The girl at the front desk was in her twenties with over-permed hair and long fingernails painted black. She glanced up, barely making eye contact, and said, "Your name?" I told her and waited. She studied the computer for an eternity before muttering in a monotone, "You passed."

The words shot through my soul like fire. I had never been so excited in my life. Now I could pursue my dream! Success, wealth, freedom, and happiness were in my grasp! I was high on life and felt like I could literally do anything.

I was blissfully unaware that all the things I dreamed about and wanted more than anything in the world would not turn out quite as I imagined.

After celebrating and shopping for a great interview outfit—and getting my real estate license, of course—I scheduled several appointments with real estate companies.

Job interviews were not exactly my specialty. I'd been a hair-stylist for the past fourteen years and owned a salon for the last seven. I had a steady clientele, but found the stylists difficult to deal with. They were always complaining, showing up late or sometimes not at all. I was ready to escape the drama of the salon world.

The first two interviews went well; so well both companies offered me positions. I didn't know then that this wasn't cause for celebration. Real estate companies give job offers to almost anyone who applies. After all, they aren't paying you anything. You work on commission, so there is low risk for the employer.

The third and final stop of the day was a well-known real estate office. I had seen their full-page ads in the newspaper. The owner walked into the reception area with a big smile and energy that seemed to bounce off the walls. He was handsome and charismatic. I followed him into a small conference room, where he leaned back in his chair with a stare so intense, he seemed to glimpse into my soul.

Without hesitating, he said, "The hardest part of this job for you will be keeping up with all the business you'll have. You will make $8,000 to $10,000 per month."

I laughed out loud and thought to myself, *Yeah, right! If I made that much money, I'd be rich!*

His face remained serious. He looked at me square in the eyes and said, "It's true. So, when would you like to start?"

As it turned out, he was telling the truth. I was a natural. Selling real estate came as instinctively to me as breathing.

I closed my first deal within forty-five days, and from there, it was like coasting downhill. I was closing multiple deals a month, adrenaline pumping through me. The proverbial money tree had sprouted from the ground and I was shaking it. Compared to the exhaustion of salon ownership, years of spending all day standing on my feet and listening to drama from stylists, it was a cakewalk. I was in my element, and there was no stopping me.

As the checks rolled in, I discovered newfound freedom, spending money however and whenever I wanted. I loved being able to buy whatever I wanted, and retail therapy became one of my favorite things.

I bought a new Lexus with every available option. I filled my home with all new furniture and started looking for a bigger and better house. I even treated my sister to a home makeover; I told her to pick out whatever she wanted. It was fun, and I was living large.

All the new "stuff" was filling up the empty spaces in my life…the spaces I didn't want to acknowledge.

The housing market was on fire, and I struggled to keep up with the amount of business coming my way.

In the process, I found myself working more and more hours. I loved what I was doing, and it seemed like realtors were expected to work all hours, night and day, so that's what I did.

After all, that's what successful people do…isn't it?

2

Love Changes Everything... Doesn't It?

Thirty-two, single, and high on my new career (and, let's be honest, money), I didn't have time to date, but you know the old saying—when you least expect it, expect it.

On a Friday afternoon, I took the rare break from work to meet a friend for happy hour.

That was the day I met my future husband. The rest is history.

One year later, we were married, and not too long after that, I was pregnant. I was still working more than ever. Money had become a drug. I couldn't make enough of it, and as a result, I was constantly chasing the high from the next big deal.

Some women float through pregnancy, they glow, they feel great. Not me—pregnancy didn't agree with me. I had never been overweight, so the extra pounds had me feeling like a giant elephant. Constantly exhausted, each day was akin to trudging through mud.

My standard thirteen-hour workdays became nearly impossible to keep up with. With the salt on the uncomfortable wound, I could no longer partake in my nightly ritual, enjoying one or two glasses of wine. All of this seriously cramped my style.

I knew I was supposed to feel differently about becoming a mom, but I couldn't help myself. I wanted that pregnancy to be over. I was ready to have the baby, regain my body, and my life pre-pregnancy. I missed the daily routine, working as many hours as I wanted to, and getting swept into the adrenaline of the next big deal.

If only someone sat me down—well, okay, given me a good slap—and talked some sense into me, maybe I would have seen nothing would ever be the same. Instead of mourning my old life, I should have been focused on myself and my child. No one did, though.

In fact, working hard is admired and encouraged. Society praises strength, perseverance.

But what about balance? We've all heard the standard spiel from flight attendants before takeoff. If there is a problem with the plane, and you're traveling with children, put your oxygen mask on first. There's much wisdom to be gleaned from this simple statement we've heard—and probably tuned out—many times. If you aren't prioritizing your own self-care, you will be in no position to help others.

Becoming a mother for the first time and still having this singular focus on work gave me pause. I wondered: *was the desire to go back to work as soon as possible normal?*

It is normal; in fact, there is a large group of women who feel, and have felt, this very way. They are part of the silent many—both men and women—who sneak back into their office after everyone has gone to bed to "catch up." The ones who never leave home without their laptop and would rather have open-heart surgery than give up their cell phone. The constantly plugged-in people who don't part with their phone, even on vacation or at a five-star restaurant. They simply *can't* unplug.

These, my friend, are the workaholics. And I was one of them.

I, like other workaholics, have a drug of choice: work.

And just like other addicts, if you look at the entire situation, you'll usually find a system of enablers surrounding the workaholic. Significant others, children, and friends accept the lifestyle. They say things like, "she's just a hard worker" or "he has a demanding career." They may complain occasionally, but over time, they get used to the behavior, and it becomes a way of life for them, too.

After the birth of my daughter, I did my best to adjust to my new lifestyle, but my priorities never changed. My career and making money remained at the top of the list. My workaholic addiction continued to dominate my life.

All I could think about was how soon I could get back to work. It ended up being six weeks. We found an in-home daycare provider to take care of our newborn daughter, and my husband and I agreed I would initially work part-time.

But, like all addicts, after I experienced just a taste of work, it wasn't enough. I needed more. I was working full time without even realizing it happened.

Coworkers and friends would make comments: "congratulations," "you must be so happy," "this is such a wonderful time in your life." I would try to smile, but inside I was struggling. It seemed like everyone who had a baby was happy except me. I was anxious, stressed, and more than anything, I just wanted to get back to work.

Writing these words is painful and embarrassing. I mean, really, what kind of mother feels this way? Like the alcoholic who wants a drink, or the sex addict lured back to a porn site, or the exercise addict who can't stay away from the gym, as a workaholic mom, the emotions and thoughts I was experiencing were actually perfectly normal. I wasn't the first who'd felt this way, and I wouldn't be the last.

I didn't share this internal struggle with anyone.

Instead, I decided I could be a great mom *and* be a rock star at my career. I could and would have it all!

As the weeks and months went by, the stress mounted, but I was a master at multi-tasking.

I told myself that I could do it all, but could I...?

3
Are You a Workaholic?

Over the years, I have learned to recognize the qualities of a workaholic. It takes one to know one, as they say. The interesting thing is society views many of these qualities as good and admirable. On the surface, you may be known as a "hard worker" or "type A."

My definition of workaholism—based on my past and observations of others like me—is simple: It's a condition where your career interferes with your life in a way that negatively affects your health and/or interpersonal relationships.

If you take note of any workaholic's life, you will find one or both areas are affected. Often, the workaholic's spouse and/

or children become codependent and therefore unconsciously support the behavior.

Here are some of the most common symptoms workaholics possess:

- Unable to relax, even when you're supposed to be off work

- Feeling unproductive and anxious if you're not working

- Drinking alcohol to relieve stress

- Not eating healthy due to (perceived) lack of time

- Not exercising due to (perceived) lack of time

- Thriving on the next big deal or promotion

- Not having any hobbies

- Not having any close friends

- Feeling isolated

- Difficulty sleeping

- Experiencing anxiety

Now that we know some symptoms, let's not dwell on the negative. Instead, let's talk about some things we can do to improve.

When I was living as a full-blown workaholic, everyone around me accepted it, celebrated it, even. I was known as a successful realtor, and that was impressive. That success was on full display from my nice home, the car I drove, the designer bags draped on my shoulder, to luxury brands of clothing I wore. You know, all the material things society tells us will make us happy.

Unfortunately, those things don't fill the void of living as a workaholic.

Looking back, if I had a few tools to help me with my addiction, I could have greatly improved not only my own life, but my family's as well.

One of the most painful aftermaths of my addiction was the time I lost with my daughter. I was not present for any of her childhood. Sure, I was there physically, if you count being in my office most of the time, but I wasn't really "there" at all. I missed so many opportunities I can never get back.

A typical day for me during what I refer to as the "lost days" would start with getting up at 7:00 a.m., working all day (sometimes I would be out showing houses or at the office), grabbing something quick for dinner—my husband did all the cooking—and taking it downstairs to my home office, where I'd usually work until midnight, sometimes later.

In the real estate business, calls and contracts come in at all hours, so I didn't have an off button. I was always on the phone trying to negotiate a real estate deal. Whatever deal I was working on at any given time seemed like the most important thing in the world; in my mind, my entire world would crash if a real estate deal fell apart.

I remember a time when my daughter was around five years old when, most evenings, she would come downstairs into my office to be with me. After all, if she didn't come down to my office, she would never see me.

I would always remind her to be quiet so I could work. She would fall asleep on the floor in her sleeping bag with our two small dachshunds on each side of her. This was a common occurrence.

Don't get me wrong, our daughter had everything she needed as far as material things go, and she was well taken care of—in fact, as an only child, she would have been considered spoiled in many ways. If she wanted a new toy, a new bike, or any other material thing, I would buy it for her. But the one thing she needed the most I couldn't give her, because I couldn't even give it to myself. I knew I had a problem, but I didn't want to face it.

I had an addiction and had no idea how to fix it.

I wish I would have had some specific tools to help me understand my behavior and how to change it, to break this cycle. Often, the behavior is subconscious, and the excuses we feed ourselves aren't the truth.

"My job is demanding."

"People just don't understand my career."

"I'll take some time off when I get caught up."

"I'm not sacrificing anything."

"My career and success are enough to fulfill me."

"I have to work hard to be successful."

Pay attention to your internal narrative. Ask yourself whether it's the truth or a fictional tale you're weaving to cover up what's truly below the surface.

Is the story you're telling yourself a cover for the areas of your life you'd rather avoid?

Tools for Life, Literally

After living many years as a workaholic, I knew I needed to make changes, *big* changes.

I achieved financial success and won numerous awards with my company. On the outside, I appeared to have it all, but the reality was, I was miserable. I had neglected my health, my family, and my life for far too long, and even the newest Gucci bag didn't bring happiness.

With a broken marriage and looming divorce, I was hiding behind my work, avoiding the inevitable. After hitting rock bottom, I visited a counselor to help me find my way through this uncharted territory.

My first meeting with Catherine was life-changing. She opened up a new world to me in ways I would have never expected. After talking about my husband and my daughter, I revealed my reason for being there. My marriage was over, and I didn't know how to leave without hurting my daughter. I was still in denial about being a workaholic, so I left that minor detail out. Catherine confidently said, "I will provide you with some tools that will help you."

I was so excited, I said, "you have tools? I need all the tools I can get!" Catherine provided some tools to assist me in navigating the demise of my marriage. She also planted the seed that I needed tools for the other areas of my life, too.

I became obsessed with this quest for tools. I was miserable and desperately needed to change. I love to read, and have always been a fan of self-help books. I read several books, but none of them gave me the prescription I craved or the tools I was seeking.

I created a list of the areas of my life I was struggling with. I wrote down eight categories: Time, Sex, Twenty Years, (I will explain this in toolbox 4) Exercise, Sleep, Vacation, Hobbies, and Friends.

One by one, I started working on these areas of my life, and in the process, I created eight virtual toolboxes designed for positive change. These toolboxes systematically changed my life for the better, and I'm confident they can do the same for you.

Back in the lost days, I wished someone would have handed me the key to unlock the door—a door I didn't even realize I needed to walk through. Lord knows I needed help. All I could see was the next deal in front of me.

As I implemented the toolboxes one by one, I started to change, my relationships started to change, and I uncovered the person I lost so many years prior. Not only did I have a life I could enjoy and be proud of, but I was making more money than ever before.

Each one of the eight toolboxes is designed to provide strategies that will help you—the workaholic—change your life. If you incorporate these toolboxes into your routine, you will experience an astonishing transformation.

Visualize a toolbox. It can be any color, any size; the important thing is to have a mental image. My toolboxes are metal, heavy, and sturdy, a dark gray color, and the titles are in large, bold, bright pink lettering centered on the front of each box. The padlocks are bright pink, too. Manifest your own unique toolboxes clearly in your mind.

Now I live in the present and am no longer a workaholic, but I still use my pink-accented toolboxes. They have become integrated into my day-to-day life. They are a habit. It doesn't take thoughtful concentration to envision them; they are just there.

But if I ever feel myself slipping back into my old ways, the workaholic inside me returning to her unhealthy habits, I pull out Toolbox One and reset.

These toolboxes changed my life. My hope and belief are they will change yours, too.

TOOLBOX 1:
Time

Imagine your first toolbox. It's solid and strong, with a padlock on it. Whatever you put in it will be safe and secure. Now imagine putting something particularly important in the toolbox: your time.

You put two hours of daily time in the box, and you must use it or lose it.

You're going to use these two hours every day, however you choose.

If you're a parent, I recommend you use one hour in your toolbox to be spent with your children. There are many things you can do, depending on their age, including reading a book, taking a walk, playing a game, or helping with homework.

I would give anything to travel back in time to when my daughter was a child. I wish I would have placed two hours in my toolbox. I would have stopped working, had dinner with her, and read her a book every night. This one simple change would have drastically changed both of our lives.

If you're not a parent, you could spend it with your spouse or significant other doing whatever you both enjoy—dinner, a walk, a massage, sex, or all of the above, and not necessarily in that order. Perhaps you need to spend time alone in a quiet place and recharge. The important thing is to be fully present.

I know this may be really difficult, but remember, you have two hours locked in the toolbox. It's safe from anybody taking it, but you must use it. All two hours. This is important —if you don't use it the same day that you place it in the box, you lose it forever. It expires at the end of each day.

If you're single, you could take a walk, exercise, take a bath, cook something nice for dinner, call a friend or family member, or make plans for a dinner or happy hour. The important thing is to use the full two hours that are in your toolbox every single day; otherwise, it's wasted and gone forever.

Here is the kicker—you must turn off your phone and your computer during these two hours. I know this part is very hard, but just do it! If you're checking messages on your phone or scrolling through Facebook, Instagram, or any other social media site, even firing off a quick email, you're not present. This two-hour reserve requires you to turn all electronics off.

It sounds simple, but it's harder than you think. As a workaholic, you will want to check a message on your phone, make a call, scroll through social media, or do the many other things that seem important or urgent.

One of the most common traits of a workaholic is believing everything has to be handled immediately. This is simply not true; an actual emergency is rare.

When you begin to apply the Time Toolbox, you may struggle to be present, turning your brain off to work, and being in the moment. But if you use it every day, doing so will become easier, and soon you will look forward to it. You will slowly change from the inside. If you're thinking you don't have two hours a day to spare because you're too busy, trust me—you can, and you must—unless you want to be like me and regret losing precious time with the people who matter the most. Time you can never, ever get back.

How will you spend your two hours? Who are the people who have been most neglected in your life? What comes to mind?

When beginning to use your Time Toolbox, maybe you need to spend it on yourself and no one else. Dig deep and be honest about how you need to use these two hours right now.

Here are some ideas you can use with the two hours in your Time Toolbox:

1. **Spend time with your child or children:** Read a book, go to the park, watch a movie, go shopping,

have dinner. Ask them what they would like to do and then honor that time, schedule the time in your day planner or on your calendar; treat it just like you would a work appointment.

2. **Take a bath, dim the lights and light a candle. Be still and calm your mind.** When was the last time you spent any time truly relaxing and allowing your mind to reset? Simply taking this time to reset and recharge can allow you to be much more productive. Place one hour in your toolbox for this time, soak in the tub, and then apply lotion to your body and relax. You may need to set boundaries with your family or spouse and let them know this time is reserved in your toolbox, and it must be used or it will expire. At first your family, friends, and/or spouse may think you have gone off the deep end, but don't worry. Soon they will see the positive changes in you. As the light in your eyes and the spark in your soul comes back, they will understand the changes you're making are the best thing that has happened to you in a very long time.

3. **Take a nap.** I know this may sound self-absorbent, but it's not. If you are sleep-deprived and overworked, let's face it—most of us are. Taking a nap may be exactly what you need. Place one hour in your toolbox, turn off the phone, close the blinds, play soft spa music, and rest. You can set the alarm

on your phone and allow yourself to doze off if you can't sleep; just relax your mind. Focus on your breathing, and every time your mind starts to race, change the thought and go back to your breathing. The goal is to quiet your mind, and you may even be able to take a nap. It may be the best thing you can do to be more productive and present in your life.

4. **Read a book.** When was the last time you read a book for pleasure? Not just a report for work, your child's homework, or an article on social media I'm talking about a book that you would like to read. If you're a reader, purchase a new book and set aside one hour to read. Find a quiet place. You may need to go outside. Wherever you choose, ensure it's a spot where you can be alone with your book.

5. **Do something fun.** That might sound far-fetched if you're drowning in work, but remember, we are only setting aside two hours a day. You can use this time one hour at a time or all at once. What sounds like fun to you? If you have been working so much you don't even remember what fun is (I've been there), here are a few ideas: meet a friend for happy hour; go shopping and buy yourself a kick-ass outfit; go out to a really nice dinner with your spouse, date, friend, or go alone; fly a kite; have a picnic; go hiking; go to the zoo; attend a movie alone and eat popcorn with lots of butter; take a walk through a park and

swing on the swing set; enjoy a bike ride; watch the sunset; have an ice cream cone; go to the farmers' market; go fishing. You could even rearrange your furniture—I know this may not sound fun, but I love to do this and it always makes me feel refreshed—I listen to music and rearrange my surroundings. There is something therapeutic about changing the flow of the room. Be open to enjoying anything else that would be fun. Eventually, you will remember what you like to do. The goal is for you to enjoy yourself, relax, and let your mind focus on something other than work.

These are just a few ideas to get you started. The important thing is to use the time in your Time Toolbox every day, or it will be gone forever—time you can never get back.

The **Time Toolbox** is very powerful; taking control of your time is life-changing. "I don't have time" won't be a part of your vocabulary anymore. You do have time and you deserve two hours a day out of twenty-four hours. Give this gift to yourself. It's so worth it and required to kick ass in life.

For me, it's easiest to schedule my two hours at the same time every day. Every evening at 7:00 p.m., I spend my two hours with my husband or a friend, or I read, write, or do something I really want to do. This is a habit now. I no longer need to consciously apply the toolbox, but it took several months to get to that point.

If my schedule does not allow for the 7:00 slot, I schedule the two hours first thing in the morning as a long walk or bike ride. I would never consider not using my two-hour time slot. I know if I don't use it, I lose it forever. I treasure my two-hour time slot and protect it because I know it's priceless.

Schedule your two hours in your planner or calendar. Take the time; I promise one day you will be grateful you did. Learning how to manage your time, and accepting that you deserve to take time off to be with your family and friends and to take care of yourself are some of the most powerful changes you can make in your life.

The Time Toolbox is a simple but powerful tool. When used consistently, it can help you shift into making time for something other than just work. Your life is bigger than your career.

You matter, your child matters, your marriage and relationships matter, your health matters—making time for these things will change everything.

4

Cracks in the Foundation

When I was in my workaholic phase of life, time flew by. I didn't exercise or eat well. I would grab whatever food was quick—and that meant gulping down fast food from a drive-through I'd eat in my car as I rushed to the next appointment.

One day, when I was about eight months pregnant, I had a listing appointment with a client across town. I had been working all day and barely had time to eat lunch, so I grabbed a protein bar and devoured it in my car.

When I finished the appointment, I began the drive home exhausted, practically falling asleep at the wheel for the hour-long trek.

The pregnancy was making it harder and harder to keep up the pace; after all, most women would be winding down at that stage in their pregnancy. But not me—I was pushing harder than ever. I wasn't taking care of myself or eating properly, and my workaholic ways were taking a toll.

After driving a few blocks, I stopped to rest my eyes for a few minutes. I was so energy-depleted, I didn't think I could make the drive. I pulled over in a residential neighborhood, turned off the car, and leaned back in the seat. It was early evening and still light out.

I woke up to a young couple knocking on my window with concerned looks. They must have been horrified; I probably looked dead!

Here I was, a very pregnant woman, passed out in the front seat of her car. I was startled and embarrassed, so I just waved, started the car, and quickly drove away. Looking back, I realize now just how dysfunctional that behavior was. I'm sharing this with you, so you can get an idea of just how detrimental an addiction to work can be to your health.

It wasn't just my physical health I was careless with; I was making and spending more money than ever, but not managing it properly. My financial health was in crisis mode, too. I had no idea where the money was going, I just knew I needed to make more. And the more I made, the more I needed, and the more I spent.

My husband and I would go on a vacation once a year, but I was on the phone and the computer the entire time. I couldn't relax. I planned the trip around whatever deal I had going at the time, arranging the trip for a time I wasn't *too* busy. I would reschedule our vacations several times before actually making it to our destination. And I never left home without my real estate files.

My relationship with my husband was on the rocks. We were completely disconnected; sex was a rarity. By the time I finished working each night, he was already in bed, and I was too tired to do anything except collapse next to him.

After many years of living in a dysfunctional marriage, using the tools Catherine provided, and armed with the courage blooming from my eight life toolboxes, I could finally follow through with the divorce. The divorce made it official, but our marriage had ended many years earlier.

Friends were shocked; they thought we had a great life and relationship. After all, we had all the material things society told us equated to happiness. Unfortunately, society lies to all of us.

Material things won't make us happy—period. End of story.

Money is essential, and we need it to live a kick-ass life, but trust me on this: If you're a workaholic, your marriage will suffer, your kids will suffer, you will suffer, and no amount of money is going to fix it. The cracks in the foundation will eventually turn into major structural problems.

In the early stages, there will be subtle signs—those fissures will start to reveal themselves. You may notice physical changes in your body, or emotional ones in your marriage, your relationship with your children, and your friendships. If ignored, the cracks will become larger and larger until the foundation is compromised and needs a major repair.

The sooner we fix the cracks in the foundation, the better off we will be. Left ignored, their effects will be too great. Without proper attention, the entire structure will crumble.

Sooner or later, you have to face the fact that life as you know it isn't working, and all the money, plaques on the wall, vehicles in the garage, and promotions aren't going to deliver the happiness you're chasing, in all the wrong places.

Look around, look closely.

Do you see any cracks in the foundation of your life?

5
Sex

A healthy sex life/intimacy are one of the key pillars of a well-rounded relationship and a requirement for a kick-ass life! Do you remember when you first met your significant other?

In the beginning stages, there was a lot of sex, right? Really good, hot sex, the kind where both people are on their best behavior, looking their best and doing their best to be a good lover. Sex is great at the beginning. When you feel sexy, the thrill of the new and unexplored is at its peak, and you both can't wait to see each other to have more of it.

Somewhere along the way, that changes. I feel safe saying that it changes for almost everyone. Maybe there are a few magical sex gods out there somehow keeping that early flame lit, but it's not the case for most of us mere mortals.

After the "hot stage" ends, we enter what I call the "comfy phase". There are some great benefits during this time, like being able to relax and be our real selves. But danger lurks here. If we aren't incredibly careful and aware, the "comfy stage" can turn into less and less sex, as we take our partner and our relationship for granted.

As a workaholic, you're even more at risk. While all relationships have the standard strains, children, money, taking each other for granted, a relationship with a workaholic adds another layer of complexity. You're way too busy and exhausted for sex, and your mind doesn't afford the proper space, being too consumed by work.

Subconsciously, you convince yourself it's okay to skip sex once in a while. After all, you're busy working and making money, and that is acceptable and even admirable. You put it off a day, and then another, until you can't remember the last time you enjoyed a passionate night of *good* sex. After all, you tell yourself, you're in a committed relationship; neither of you is going anywhere or needs to prove how hot you are. You're past that stage.

Before you know it, you aren't having sex at all. Now you've entered the danger zone. If you're not having sex or intimacy your relationship is in trouble.

Obviously, if there is a medical or other underlying reason for not having sex, that's different. There are other ways to be intimate, even just setting aside time to be alone together, holding hands, and touching. Sex and physical touch are some of the most important things to keep couples connected.

Touch is powerful; as humans, we all need to be touched. Not only is sex and intimacy important to achieving a stronger and healthier relationship, sex or even a simple hug releases endorphins in our brain. These endorphins relax us, improve our mood, and have many science-backed benefits to improving our mental well-being.

Sex and intimacy are required to have a healthy kick-ass life. So, let's explore the Sex Toolbox.

TOOLBOX 2

Sex

Your Sex Toolbox holds a place for you to be intimate with your spouse or significant other. Here, you're going to reserve time just for sex and intimacy. Remember, the box is locked, and the time is there for you to use. You must use it—only for sex and intimacy—or it will expire, and you will lose it forever.

Start by thinking about sex. Yes, you heard that right, just *thinking* about sex. Place ten minutes per day in your toolbox to visualize sex. Do this for seven days straight.

It should go without saying, but be sure to think about good/hot sex. Visualize the details. You may have to travel back in your memories to the "hot stage" in your relationship or marriage if it's a bit stale.

In that case, remember how you used to feel when you were getting dressed for a date, where you went, and where you were when you had sex. Think about how you felt when you touched each other and how turned on you both were. Visualize having sex with your partner when you were in the "hot stage."

After seven days, you should start to feel more sexual. You may even begin to miss the intimacy you once shared with your spouse or significant other. The goal is to wake up those dormant sexual thoughts. They are still there; they are just asleep.

Unfortunately, they may have snoozed for so long they seem to be down for the count. Don't despair—your sexual desire is there. You just need to awaken it. Dedicating these ten minutes a day is the first step in the process.

On the eighth day, place time in your toolbox for sex (and/ or intimacy) two times a week, two hours per session. If you're already having sex two times a week or more, you're ahead of the curve. Instead, use some of that focused time to open a safe dialogue with your partner about sex. This gives you both the opportunity to find ways—together— how to improve that time.

You've spent the week visualizing what you want. Now is the time to share it and learn what your partner would also like more of. But if you're a workaholic, I suspect you're having very little sex, if any at all.

Time to spice up that sex life!

The idea of scheduling time for sex may not sound very romantic, but it's necessary. Otherwise, it won't happen; we already know that.

If you're not having any sex, two hours twice per week may feel like a lot of time to set aside for it. If it's too much for you initially, progress at your own pace. Or maybe sex does not seem possible at all.

If it's been a long time since you have been intimate with your spouse or significant other, it may not be realistic to jump into bed, even after your week of sex visualization. Listen to your body and follow your instincts. Give each other a massage or hold hands. Or simply just be present together. Do whatever feels best. To reconnect physically is an excellent starting point.

We are all different, and there are many underlying factors, so please just use this time how it works for you. You will be amazed at how much better you feel, and your relationship will transform.

I once heard a radio program that stuck with me. A relationship therapist was talking about a couple on the verge of divorce. This couple started counseling, and after six months, they were ready to move forward with the divorce. The therapist asked them if they would be willing to try an experiment before deciding to separate. The experiment was to have sex every day for thirty days, no matter what—even if one or both were not in the mood. The only excuse they could use to skip sex was a physical reason, like illness. The couple reluctantly agreed to try it out.

In the beginning, it was difficult. Both were angry at the other; they were disconnected and hadn't had sex for many months prior. In fact, they had been sleeping in different rooms. Having sex was the last thing either wanted. But each day, they pushed forward.

After a couple of weeks, they were making jokes about sex, laughing together, and enjoying the renewed intimacy. They were reconnecting, both physically and emotionally. By the end of the thirty days, they realized they did still love each other and decided not to get a divorce. They were both committed to working on the issues in their marriage.

Obviously, sex isn't the be-all and end-all to solve all relationship problems, but it's important and needs to be in one of your toolboxes.

Here are some ideas how you can add some spice to your sex life:

1. **Sit in a hot tub or take a bath together.** Relax, spend time in your bedroom without the expectation of having sex. You can discuss this together ahead of time to set the expectation and take the pressure off. Talk in bed and touch each other, cuddle and just be still together. Remember how it felt to be intimate in this way.

2. **Give each other a massage—**use quality massage oils and light a candle, enjoy a glass of wine or herbal tea, and take your time. If you feel sexual

and want to have sex, that is awesome, but I would recommend you both initially agree this time is for reconnecting without sex. Several of my girlfriends have shared they often feel their husband wants to have sex with no connection or foreplay. They aren't in the mood, and it eventually becomes another chore they feel obligated to do, stripping sex of all enjoyment. By giving each other a massage, you can connect physically and start to rebuild your desire for sex. You can purchase a massage table or just enjoy your bed. The main thing is to touch and relax. Spruce up your bedroom with new bedding, buy new sheets and a new comforter, add a new candle, hang a new painting—changing your environment is a great way to freshen up your space and make it more inviting.

3. **Reconnect with your sexual self.** If you're not feeling sexy in your skin, it's difficult to want to have sex with anyone. Focus on the qualities you like about yourself, and decide you will accept and love your body as is. Remind yourself daily that your body has changed due to childbirth, menopause, age, stress, or whatever has led you off track to feeling less sexual. It is interesting that menopause is also known as "the change of life." Clearly, we change physically when we go through menopause, and yet we somehow expect ourselves to be the same sexy person. This applies to any change your body

has gone through. Maybe you had surgery and your body and physical endurance haven't returned. Give yourself a break; accept that you're a beautiful, strong person who has overcome a lot. You're a badass and your stretch marks, baby weight, wrinkles, and everything else that makes you who you are, are what makes you strong and beautiful.

Do something to feel good about yourself. It could be getting your hair cut and highlighted, buy a new outfit, buy a new pair of shoes that are sexier than you would typically wear, buy a new pair of panties and bra, buy a new nightgown, get spray-tanned, take an exercise class, buy your spouse flowers or a piece of jewelry. Think about sex—find that spark inside; it's there! Be kind to yourself and don't be critical of your body. You're beautiful, strong as hell, and your man loves you. For the men reading this, find your mojo by remembering that you're a strong, sexy man, and your partner loves you.

4. **Go for it!** If it's physically possible and there are no medical reasons why you can't have sex, just do it. The interesting thing about sex is the more you have, the more you want. Sex is good for you and your relationship and can bring you closer in so many ways. Obviously, this does not apply to everyone, and every situation is different. If it works for you, and you can have sex that feels right, have sex at least two times a week. The time will be in your Sex

Toolbox, and you will look forward to it. The more, the merrier!

One of the most challenging things to do in a relationship is to keep sex fresh. It's human nature for things to slow down the longer you're together, and as we age, sex seems to slow down, too. If you're aware of this, and stay committed to your Sex Toolbox, you can avoid this!

Try new things, new positions, and new locations. I'm sure you've heard the term "vacation sex." Why do we have better sex when we are on vacation? Maybe because we are relaxed and we actually make time for sex. We're in a new environment, sex feels different and new, making it more exciting. We can create the same thing by having sex in various locations in our house. Be open to new experiences with your partner. The most important thing is to stay connected sexually and intimately.

One of my favorite books is *The Five Love Languages* by Gary Chapman. This book explains how we all experience love uniquely and details the different ways we need to feel loved. By understanding your loved one's love language, you can provide what they need to be fulfilled in a relationship.

The first time I read the book, I was fascinated to learn what my love languages were. I realized that if I had known my ex-husband's love language, I would have recognized early on how out of sync we were. This book is an excellent read and can enrich your relationships.

Make time to invest in your sexual relationship. It's a powerful way to stay connected with your significant other and in tune with your sexual energy.

Even if you're not currently in a relationship, know that you will attract your soulmate eventually, and the skills you learn now will be valuable. Physical touch is important to our well-being and is required for a kick-ass life.

Important Caveat: If you're in an unhealthy or abusive relationship, use the time in your toolbox to meet with a therapist. Everybody's situation is unique, and my suggestions are not to be confused with that of a qualified medical professional.

6

Regrets

I t was 7:00 a.m., and the sun was shining through at the edges of the closed curtains. I rolled over and remembered I was on vacation. The getaway I'd planned months prior had finally arrived. We were in Maui and staying at the Grand Wailea, one of the most exclusive resorts on the island. I'd dreamed of coming here for years.

I had worked hard for months with no days off and desperately needed a vacation. My body ached, and I had a slight headache from too many hours hunched in front of a computer; I spent the entire flight working while my family slept.

Quietly climbing out of bed, I headed for the hotel coffee maker. As the coffee brewed, I glanced at my cell phone. I collected my fresh cup of coffee and phone and tiptoed out to the balcony, trying not to wake my family.

Before I even took a sip, an email caught my attention. The real estate deal I had been working on for months was in jeopardy. There was an inspection issue threatening the entire deal. I had someone covering for me, but this was too big for anyone else to handle. I needed to step in—and *fast.*

I sent a quick email to my fellow agent. One led to another, and before I knew it, I was in full-on work mode.

My daughter was awake now and ran out to the balcony with a big smile on her face. "Mommy, we're here! Look at the water, it's so pretty! Can we go to the beach?" She was loud and excited.

I quickly snapped, "Not now. I have to make a call. Keep your voice down!"

The look in her eyes should have brought me back to reality. Instead, I turned my attention back to my phone and made the call.

I spent almost that entire vacation working. When I wasn't working, I was thinking about it. At the end of each day, I drank to relax.

I was in one of the most beautiful places in the world, and I didn't create one amazing memory.

Not one.

This was a typical vacation for me in the lost days. Now, I vacation every three months and am entirely present for the duration of every trip; with the goal being to create as many memories as possible.

As soon as I leave, I turn my business over to an associate. Problems may arise, but they can handle them. I'm no longer afraid to release control and have ditched the belief that no one can handle things as well as I can.

How I wish it hadn't taken me so long to learn this lesson...

What if you could go on a vacation and not work the whole time? In fact, what if you didn't work at all? What if you could be fully present in the moment, experience and enjoy the people you're with? What if you could truly relax?

These things may be hard to imagine, but you can do them, and if you do, your whole outlook on life will change.

Now, let's explore the Planning and Taking a Vacation Toolbox. One of my favorites!

TOOLBOX 3:

Planning and Taking a Vacation

Planning a vacation is part of the fun of going. It's exciting to picture yourself in the location you've always dreamed about visiting, right?

In your Vacation Toolbox is one hour per week, which you will spend planning a vacation until you have formed the perfect one. You can spend this hour in the morning before you start your day or in the evening (I don't recommend planning your vacation during working hours, because you will be distracted).

Now, reserve fourteen days per year to actually take a vacation. You can use these fourteen days however you like, one week at a time, long weekends, or one trip that lasts fourteen days. However, you have to use **all** fourteen days.

After choosing the location, dates, and details, book the vacation and place it in your toolbox. Know that it's locked and secure and waiting for your departure.

As the trip approaches, go back and look at the details often. Plan out any additional activities you want to do while you're there and visualize yourself doing these activities. Remind yourself constantly that you deserve this trip—that this time of relaxation is one of the reasons you work so hard.

You may start to feel anxious about going as you get closer to the departure date. After all, work is so busy, how can you get away? The timing just isn't right. You may even consider canceling, but remember...your trip is locked in the toolbox. You're going!

Find a colleague to cover for you while you're gone and brief them on everything you have in the pipeline. Leave an out-of-office voicemail on your phone and an auto-reply on your email. Your message must say that you will be out of town and won't have access to email or phone, and provide the name and contact information for the person who they can contact during your absence. Make it clear that you won't be responding to any communication until your return. Knowing that you have set these expectations should relieve some pressure.

Above all, don't get caught up in the power trip that no one else can do what you do, or that they won't do it correctly. That is a power trip that won't serve you well.

Everyone is replaceable. **Everyone.**

If the company you work for won't approve your time off or does not properly value an unplugged vacation, then it is time to reevaluate your career choice and consider a change. Time off from work is required to have a kick-ass life.

When you arrive at your destination, remind yourself of the rules: you won't be checking texts or emails, you're unplugged and on vacation mode. In fact, tell yourself every day that you deserve a vacation, and it's perfectly acceptable to take work-free vacations.

Successful people take vacations, including presidents, CEOs, surgeons, attorneys, real estate agents, mothers, fathers, and anyone else you can think of. You can, too!

Stick to the plan you created for each day. Try new activities, but listen to your body. If you're tired, rest, eat healthy food, and treat yourself to a massage or spa service. If you like to read, find time in the day to read something enjoyable.

The first time you go on a vacation and don't work at all will be a life-changing experience. At least, it was for me.

You deserve to recharge, and when you go back to work feeling renewed, you will be much more productive. You will kick more ass than you ever thought possible. The more you take care of your body, mind, and soul, the more you will achieve.

Believe it or not, taking time off will make you more productive at work. At the same time, it will position you for promotions and the potential for greater financial earnings. This was an earth-shattering lesson for me.

I love to travel, so my Vacation Toolbox always has at least one trip inside. As I have gotten better at traveling and trusting that I deserve to vacation and that taking time off improves my productivity, I plan my trips for the entire year, starting in January. I enjoy knowing they are in the toolbox, safe and secure. Throughout the year, I remind myself that I have vacations to look forward to. This serves as a reminder as to why I work so hard.

Reward yourself with a wonderful vacation. It doesn't have to be expensive; you can go camping or hiking, rent a cabin in the woods or a beach house, or schedule a girls' weekend.

The point is to plan it, show up, and be present. Create memories you will cherish forever. Here are some ideas for your vacation toolbox:

1. **Plan a girls' trip.** Research locations that sound fun and relaxing. Maybe you want to go to Vegas for the weekend and catch a show, Or how about a spa vacation? Or stay in town and go to a nice hotel with a pool, drink mimosas, sleep in and watch old movies or chick flicks?

2. **A romantic weekend with your spouse or hot date.** If you have children, get a babysitter. Try a bed-and-breakfast in New England, a ski trip to the Colorado mountains, or a beach vacation to Mexico.

3. **Plan a trip alone.** Select a location that soothes your soul. Maybe it's a cute cabin in the mountains or a yoga retreat. When you arrive, turn off your phone and unplug your life. Take naps, indulge yourself with delicious, healthy meals, take a bubble bath and read that book that has been on your nightstand for several months (or years).

4. **Leave the country.** Europe, Australia, South America, Asia...it's a big world out there! Research the places you want to see and the things you can do when you're there. Do you like history? Check out local museums and historical sites. Hiking? Go for a hike in a rain forest or up a mountain. If you're the adventurous type, snowmobile on a glacier, scuba-dive in caves. The possibilities are endless. Follow your soul to your next adventure!

Maui is one of my favorite places and never disappoints. Wherever you go, select your travel partners carefully. Make sure you're comfortable with the people you're traveling with. Plan out your itinerary for each day and include "rest days."

5. Staycation. If travel isn't your thing, schedule your time off and enjoy a staycation at home, stock your home with delicious food and watch movies, read, take walks, take a nap, ride your bike. Do all the things you enjoy but never have time to do when you're working. A staycation can be a great way to recharge without going anywhere.

Visit your Vacation Toolbox often prior to your trip to stay excited!

Reward yourself with vacations. It's an excellent way to create memories that you will treasure for a lifetime and it's an important part of kicking ass in your life!

7

Take a Chance While You Have One

As I've gotten older, I realize how fragile life is. Time passes so quickly, and we aren't promised tomorrow. Opportunities come and go.

When I look at the people in my life whom I respect and admire, I see they have interesting lives. They have gone to places I want to go; they have seen things I want to someday see. They are successful and have enough money to do these things. They enjoy the money they have.

What good is money if you don't enjoy it? If all you do is save for retirement, what happens if you don't make it to retirement? Which, by the way, happens all the time.

If you really want a new home but are afraid to buy it because you're fearful the real estate market may decline or crash completely, let me put it this way: Not only will you miss out if the market escalates, but you'll miss out on the experience of living in the home you long to live in, the home you have worked so hard to purchase.

There are no guarantees, so take a chance. Live your life the way you feel called to. In my real estate career, I have witnessed many people miss out on opportunities because they were afraid to take a chance.

One particular person who clings to my memory was a VP for a large corporation; we'll call him Tom. Tom had searched high and low for his dream home and finally hired me as his buyer's agent to help him find it. I was on a mission. I never missed a new listing; I searched the market daily and worked my network for off-market properties.

Tom himself spent hours and hours over the span of months, scouring the internet for new listings. And then, one morning, there it was—the home he had searched for, dreamed of, was on the market! We promptly scheduled a showing to beat the competition. This was a special home, and the market was strong. I knew it would sell quickly.

The moment he stepped through the front door; Tom's eyes lit up. As we walked through each room, he became more and more excited. I had never seen him so taken by a property. After touring, he looked at me with his eyes glistening and said, "I love it."

While I knew this was his dream home, I also knew he could afford it. As a high-salary executive, he could easily pay cash, but was pre-approved for a mortgage. I was certain he would want to move forward. I mean, this was it! This home had everything Tom had been looking for; it was the home that was so difficult to find.

Tom and I made eye contact while standing in the living room in front of the enormous windows that framed an exquisite view. I asked, "Would you like me to prepare the contract?"

Shuffling his feet, Tom looked away and replied, his voice tense. "Let me think about it. I'll get back to you tomorrow."

I was surprised but understood it was a big decision, and sleeping on it seemed reasonable.

The next morning, I received a call from the listing agent. She was following up on the showing and asked me for feedback. I explained that the buyer was interested and was considering an offer. The listing agent informed me that they had six more showings scheduled for that same day, and there was significant interest in the property. I asked her to keep me informed should another offer come in.

I have never been a hard-sell agent; in fact, I don't even like the word "sell." I don't believe in pushing anything on anybody.

Tom hadn't reached out to me all morning. By noon, I decided I should follow up. At a minimum, he needed to know what the listing agent shared about the scheduled showings and interest in the property.

When he answered the phone, he sounded distant, not like his usual friendly self. I told him about the interest in the property, but he cut the conversation short and ended the call with, "I'm still thinking about it, I'll get back to you."

I knew then that Tom was talking himself out of buying his dream home, that fear was taking over. For whatever reason, he didn't think he deserved his dream home; he was not allowing himself to take a chance.

From experience, I knew there was nothing I could do or say. We all have our own belief systems, and we act accordingly. Until we can change the narratives we tell ourselves, we will continue to repeat the same patterns over and over again.

By the end of the day, there was still no word from Tom. The listing agent called at five that evening. "We have accepted a full-price cash offer. Thank you for your interest." Just like that, my buyer's dream home was gone.

He had the money, he loved the home, he wanted it more than anything in the world, and he had worked for many years to afford it, but he couldn't pull the trigger.

Fear and a deep-seated belief that he didn't deserve it robbed Tom of his dream home. This has happened time and again, to several of my clients.

Follow your gut and do what makes you happy. There will be opportunities that come your way, but it's up to you to act on them. If you can kick ass at work, you can kick ass in your life, too.

After all, isn't your life more important than any job?

Or, for that matter, more important than anything else you have?

Now, let's explore the Twenty Years Toolbox, which will help you gain clarity on how you want your life to look in the future and become crystal clear on the memories you would like to create.

TOOLBOX 4
Twenty Years

The Twenty Years Toolbox is used in a slightly different way. You're going to use this toolbox as if you're in the future, reflecting on the past twenty years of your life.

Start by placing the next twenty years of your life in the toolbox.

You will have a virtual toolbox and a physical memory box. The virtual toolbox is where you will visualize the memories you want to see in your future; the physical memory box is where you will store pictures, cards, letters, and keepsakes of the memories as you create them. This can be a physical toolbox that you make, or a folder on your computer titled "Twenty Years."

Making your memory box is a fun craft project that you can utilize for your Hobby Toolbox. (toolbox 7) This visualization exercise is like looking into a crystal ball, which shows you the future.

The box has been locked for twenty years. You're standing in the future, and it's the day you open it.

During those twenty years, you probably set goals and worked to achieve those goals. But regardless of what those goals were, regardless of your successes and mistakes, regardless of everything you did and didn't do—the time has passed.

I recommend you revisit this toolbox once a month. By regularly visualizing your life as though twenty years have passed, you will be reminded of what is important to you.

So, open the box and consider its contents. Given that you're twenty years into the future, how old are you now? How old are your children? Are you retired or close to retirement? Are the people you love—especially older family members such as your parents—still with you?

What can you manifest in this toolbox that will make your heart sing? How can you sum up the last twenty years? What did you do? Did you take any amazing trips, like Europe or some other place you've always wanted to visit? What were the highlights of the years?

Maybe your child got married and you were seated in the front row at the wedding. You tried not to cry, but the tears seeped from the corners of your eyes. Or your child graduated from high school or college while you sat in the audience, beaming with pride.

Maybe, further back in those twenty years, you can remember them playing in the backyard or starring in an elementary school play. Perhaps you yourself got married, and you can still visualize the details of your wedding day and feel the happiness of the day. Within those twenty years, you met the love of your life and had your first kiss.

Did you buy the beach house you always dreamed of? Can you see yourself there, creating memories with those you love? These types of memories are what you will find in your toolbox.

Now look at the present time. Does that pressing matter at work seem so important? The promotion you're working so hard to get—will it even matter? The ten or twenty pounds you're trying to lose; do you care if you didn't? That big sale you're about to close—will it make the cut for your toolbox? The trial you're working on twelve hours a day that seems like the most important thing in the world—will that be an accomplishment you treasure?

What parts of your life will you cherish forever?

For most of us, especially if our health has declined or we've lost loved ones in those twenty years, material possessions will be the farthest thing from our minds.

Of course, we all need to make money. Being successful is wonderful, but it's not the most important or the only thing. The memories and moments you create now are what will matter most in the future, and if you don't take time to create them, you may discover the bitter reality of regret.

Don't let that happen to you.

This toolbox holds your visualizations of what you would like those cherished memories to be. Most people never take the time to picture what their life will look like twenty years from now.

Sure, we think and plan for retirement, investing in our 401K, working toward paying off our mortgage. But this is different. This exercise is about applying the skill of visualizing the memories you hope to create.

Think about the memories and experiences you want to see when you open your toolbox and write them down—add more items to this list as you create memories and envision new ones.

Here are some ideas to help get you started with your own Twenty Years Toolbox:

1. **Love.** Yes, love is beautiful and very important to find in your toolbox. Love has to be earned and nurtured, just like everything else important to us. Take the time and effort to focus on your relationships, so you will be surrounded by love when you open your toolbox.

2. **Memories with your loved ones.** If you have children, seeing the memories you created will be priceless. You will cherish the memories with your children, school plays, sports games, birthday parties, weddings, and the many other life events.

If you worked all the time and missed many of those years, they are gone, and they won't be in your toolbox. I'm passionate about making a point here because I missed so many years with my daughter. I can never get those back. I thought my career was more important—and that was a mistake I can never reverse. I can, however, be there for the remaining years and use those to create memories.

If you want to travel and see the world, plan it and make it happen. Make sure that the memory of you in the south of France with a smile and a sparkle in your eye is in your toolbox (or wherever your heart desires).

We have the power to create our future. There is plenty of time to work and make money, and we need to make money so we can afford to go to the south of France. Just don't sacrifice memories and time with your loved ones working to pay for that trip.

3. **A picture tells a story.** As the years pass, the dates and years for your adventures will fade. When you're creating the memories for your future, make sure you label pictures chronologically. Start a file with the date and year, so you can easily reflect and remember.

Place pictures in your physical memory toolbox. Save them to your "Twenty Years" folder on your computer or, better yet, create your own hands-on toolbox. More on this when we get to the hobby toolbox.

4. **Letters and Cards.** Your Twenty Years Memory Toolbox is an excellent place to store letters and cards from your loved ones. What a beautiful gift to open your toolbox and find these memories! If you receive a special card from a loved one, place it in your memory toolbox. Someday these letters and cards will be more meaningful than they are today.

Use your Twenty Years physical and memory toolboxes to conceptualize your future and to preserve those memories. This can be one of the most powerful tools you have to ensure the future you desire and will treasure.

8
Every Picture Tells a Story

I n the lost days, I wasn't taking care of myself and therefore didn't look well.

The lack of exercise, working night and day, not eating well, drinking too much, no sex, and low-grade depression were taking a toll. In short, I looked like hell! I'd gained twenty pounds and started wearing frumpy clothes. I'd colored my long, bright blonde hair to a dark ashy blonde and cut it above my shoulders, telling myself I needed to look more professional.

I had lost myself—the real me had slipped away. My workaholic addiction had taken a toll, and it showed.

I've always loved Rod Stewart's song "Every Picture Tells a Story." It's so true. Have you ever looked at a picture of yourself and thought, *WTF? That can't be me!?* Maybe you gained a few pounds but talked yourself into believing you should squeeze into those short shorts. A picture is a reality check that requires you to literally *see* yourself.

I have a picture of myself in the lost days. I named it "scary Paula;" I keep it on my desktop and refer to it on occasion. It's important for me to remember how lost (and how scary) I really was, and how far I have come.

My then-husband had the camera and took the picture at a beautiful resort next to a lake. I'm posing with my daughter, who is around six years old.

I'm wearing black stretch pants and a bright pink shirt, and my hair is pulled back in a ponytail. My face is puffy with a reddish tone (too much wine, not enough rest), and I'm about twenty pounds heavier than I'm now (that's where the stretch pants come in), and my eyes are flat.

Yep, flat. No sparkle at all.

I remember that vacation and that very moment when the picture was snapped. I was in a beautiful place with my family, yet having a miserable time. Constantly working, per usual, and I was not taking care of myself.

When I look at that picture, I wish I could go back and give my lost self the eight toolboxes. I would tell her that life does not have to be all about work and money and that hiding behind her career while not dealing with the real issues in her life will cause the foundation to crack and heave. I would explain that it's possible to have both success and happiness.

Looking at that picture, I hardly recognize the person I was. I was lost in the fog of a workaholic lifestyle. I had become a shell of myself, an unhappy, lost soul.

My divorce was an awakening. I realized if I ever wanted to meet someone whom I could have a healthy relationship with, I was going to have to start dating. This was a scary thought. My self-esteem was low, and I could barely look in the mirror.

I decided to start exercising and apply my Exercise Toolbox. I bought a treadmill and walked thirty minutes a day. Thirty minutes led to forty-five, and then to an hour. Next, I joined a nearby gym and started taking spinning and weight-lifting classes. I could feel myself changing from the inside out.

Twenty pounds lighter, I colored my drab hair color back to blonde and went shopping. I replaced almost all the clothes in my closet, which looked like they belonged to someone else, someone I didn't know and couldn't relate to at all. After that, I looked and felt like a new person.

I was finding myself—the person I'd lost many years before. Clients who hadn't seen me for a few years almost didn't recognize me. Losing twenty pounds was a perk of exercise, but the true benefit was the shift in my mindset.

Here is a secret: don't get hung up on weight and numbers on the scale—just focus on self-care and the health benefits of exercise.

After I started exercising, I also changed my eating habits and stopped drinking alcohol during the week. Because I was working out, it just didn't feel right to eat the wrong foods and drink too much. It was a natural transition.

Exercise changes everything. It *must* be incorporated into your life. I can hear it now, "I don't have time." Here's the thing, you *do* have time, and it will be well spent. Stick with me.

Now, let's explore the Exercise Toolbox.

TOOLBOX 5:

Exercise

Using the Exercise Toolbox, you will allow yourself time and effort to take care of your body.

The old story we have been telling ourselves goes something like this: "I don't have time to exercise."

Or this: "My knees hurt; I just can't exercise."

Or this: "I'll start next week when I get caught up at work."

Stories like these no longer fit in our life. They are outdated and do not serve us anymore.

Imagine yourself fit and healthy; a time in your life when you were healthier than you are now. Did you feel better about yourself? Have more energy?

We are all critical of ourselves, I know that. So, I'm not suggesting that you look for perfection, just a time when you were exercising on a regular basis or generally taking care of yourself physically.

If you have never been one to exercise, and have never felt healthy, or have never had a fit and healthy image of yourself, imagine what it would be like to feel good in your skin.

Not perfection, not a number on a scale, not a certain clothing size—just *healthy.*

Find a picture of an activity you would like to incorporate into your exercise routine. Search online for ideas of an activity that appeals to you. This can be anything from a bike ride or walking. Don't get caught up in the picture of a "perfect" person; just find something physical that resonates with you.

Print a copy of the activity and post it at your desk. Look at this picture every day for seven days to build up the desire to be in shape. Every day, visualize yourself doing this activity and *feel* yourself taking better care of your body and allowing time to get healthy.

This desire, this growing emotion, is important. It will jump-start your exercise routine.

Each morning when you look at the photo, brainstorm what type of exercise you will commit to in order to *feel* like you want to exercise. You may already know what activity you can commit to. Do you belong to a gym, or have a treadmill in your house, or do you enjoy dancing? Whatever it is, think about an exercise you can and will do.

It may be as simple as taking a walk around the block, a yoga class, or dancing in your living room. It really doesn't matter what it is; just decide you can and will commit to doing it. Don't overcomplicate this decision.

On the eighth day, place your chosen exercise into your toolbox and devote thirty minutes a day to it. That's all... just thirty minutes once a day. Know that the time in your box is safe and set aside. You must use it every day, or you will lose it.

If you want to exercise longer, you can—but thirty minutes a day is the minimum required. The most important thing is to be consistent. You may tell yourself you don't have time, but you do. You just have to make exercise a habit, like brushing your teeth.

Exercise is one of the best things you can do to jump-start improving your life. Making time for yourself to exercise will set the pace for the rest of your life.

There are many reasons to exercise, including improving your health, state of mind, appearance, and self-esteem. One of the most significant benefits is the message you send to your subconscious and the universe. When you make time to exercise, you tell yourself that you are worth it and that you matter—that you are as important as that real estate deal or that report or that litigation you're working on. The message you are sending to your subconscious is powerful and will flow into the other important areas of your life.

With these thirty minutes a day, with each stride or pedal of the bike or lift of the weights, your life will change. When you begin to add regular exercise to your life, you will also want to eat healthy; the two go hand in hand. After exercising, you won't be as tempted to grab that donut. It just won't feel right.

Start adding healthy foods to the cart when you go shopping. Buy fresh vegetables and organic foods.

I have never been a fan of "diets" to lose weight. The problem for me with a diet is I can only do it for so long, and then I stop and revert back to my eating habits. I also feel like diets come from scarcity, and living in a state of scarcity does not work for me. We are more successful if we come from a place of abundance.

If you feel called to feed your body in a healthy way with quality delicious food, and you honor this, you will have a much higher success rate than any strict diet. By creating new habits, you eliminate the risk of failing.

Listen to your body and eat the foods that make you feel good and that your body responds to favorably.

For me, I have learned my body does not process carbs and gluten well. If I eat carbs and gluten products, I gain weight, feel lethargic, and am not at my best. It's that simple. I also avoid sugar, except for the sugar in wine—a girl has to have her priorities! I believe in enjoying life. An extremely restrictive diet isn't for me.

Eating well and exercising are crucial to a healthy, balanced life.

You *can* commit to both, even if you don't think so right

now.

I used to dread working out. Now, it's one of my favorite parts of the day. It's my time to reset and clear my mind.

When I return to work afterward, I'm more productive and make better decisions. Applying the Exercise Toolbox is one of the most productive things you can do.

Another trap to avoid is getting caught up in other people's progress. It's so easy these days. Six-packs and toned bodies bombard us everywhere we look—from television, to movies, to social media. Someone else's weight or fitness level is personal to them, just as your health journey is personal to you.

Stay true to your individual progress. If you can only walk to the end of the driveway, that's great! Add a few steps each day and keep going.

If you can only walk fifteen minutes on the treadmill, congratulate yourself for committing to exercise and add a few minutes each day.

Above all, be kind to yourself and remember you can do this!

If the idea of finding time to exercise seems ludicrous because your planner is already overflowing...you're in the right place!

When I was a workaholic, I was 100% sure I didn't have

time to exercise. I would have bet my life there was no way I could fit it in. I was so busy I was lucky to take a shower most days.

Let's start with the word *busy* We all have the same amount of time in the day—it's our choice how we fill those hours. If we are working eighteen hours out of twenty-four, we choose this. If we spend twelve hours sleeping, this is also a choice we've made.

The truth is, we make time for things important to us. If your job is the most important thing to you, you will set aside as much time needed for it.

When you decide exercise is important and must be included in your life, you will make time to exercise. It really is that simple.

In the Exercise Toolbox, we are placing thirty minutes in the toolbox every day. If you set it for the same time, it will be easier to stay committed. You can set your morning alarm earlier or stop working thirty minutes earlier to fit this in.

I recommend scheduling all of the exercise blocks of time for the entire week on Sunday. Schedule this time just as you would an appointment for work, decide right now that you will honor this time. A strong body and clear mind are a powerful combination to achieve a kick-ass life.

Here are some ideas to get you started on your Exercise Toolbox:

1. **Find a picture of yourself when you felt good in your skin.** The picture should bring a good vibe when you look at it. Please don't get hung up on your weight or size, just find a picture of yourself you like. Place the picture where you can see it and look at it every day. Use it as a motivator.

I was cleaning out my closet this week and found an entire drawer of shorts I don't wear anymore because they are too small. I kept them in case I could fit in them again. I decided it was silly to hold on to them since they were too small; I told myself I should accept the fact I'll never fit in them again. As I started to bag them up, one pair caught my eye. I picked them up and took a closer look. They were so cute. I remembered buying them a few years back. I looked at the waist size and thought, "damn, I was in great shape."

That's when I decided NOT to get rid of them. Then I took a look at the rest of my short collection and decided to keep them all. The shorts were motivation, a reminder that I can fit in them again if it's important to me. Now the beige shorts that I love are in my office where I can see them every day. They are hanging on my book shelf, and I can't walk into my office without noticing them. I may not ever fit into my beige shorts with the shiny buttons again, and that is okay—they are a reminder of a time in my life when I was healthy and in great physical shape. That motivates me to keep working out every day and to be my best self. Find something you can look at that will evoke that same motivation within you.

2. **Find an exercise that you like.** That sounds simple, but if you haven't been working out for a while, you may not be sure what to try. You could take a walk in your neighborhood or in a nearby park. I recommend tracking your steps and try to increase them as you progress.

Dance in your living room or ride your bike. You could find an in-person class like spin, water aerobics, or yoga. If you feel more comfortable working out at home, there are options available to you there too.

I purchased a Peloton bike. I love my bike; the classes are better than any class I ever took at the gym. I don't have to leave my house, and that saves time. Plus, I can look as bad as I want to and no one will know. There are online classes available for everything from weight training to yoga. Find something that works for you!

3. **Don't be critical of yourself.** It's perfectly fine if you are only able to walk to the end of the street; add a few more steps the next day. Be kind to yourself; taking the first step is enough to change your routine and make exercise part of your life. Write down your

goals and place that in your Exercise Toolbox. Label a file on your computer called Exercise Toolbox. Write down your current weight and measurements along with the date, list the exercise you're committing to, and the schedule you will follow. Check in once a month and see how you're doing as you move forward. Celebrate your success! Treat yourself to a massage or spa day as a reward for committing to your Exercise Toolbox.

4. **Jazz up your workout clothing.** I work out at home, so no one sees me except my husband, but I have made a habit of updating my workout clothes. When I purchase new workout gear, I feel more motivated to work out because I want to wear them. Make sure your exercise clothes fit you properly, too. This makes a difference in how you feel. If they are too tight, replace them with clothes that fit and that you can move comfortably in.

This applies to *all* your clothing. Wearing clothes that are too tight isn't good for your self-esteem and creates a low-grade energy. If you need a larger size, update your wardrobe. When clothes fit properly, you look good *and* feel good.

The single most important thing is to just do it! Place the thirty minutes a day in your toolbox and make it happen. I'm willing to bet you spend thirty minutes a day doing things that don't really add any benefit to your life; scrolling on social media, watching TV, and worrying about things that really don't matter.

These thirty minutes will change your life.

This isn't about being a certain size or trying to be perfect, it's about taking care of yourself, body, and mind. You take care of everyone and everything else, now it's time to take of yourself.

You deserve this time, and you can do it.

You will feel yourself changing with each step.

I promise!

Be kind to yourself and remember you can do this!

9

No Sleep for the Weary

It was midnight. With blurred vision, I logged out of my computer and took another sip of wine.

I knew I needed to get to sleep. Tomorrow was another big day. With an early morning closing and an afternoon filled with showings, I needed to be on my game.

I tiptoed into the bedroom, trying not to wake my daughter, who was asleep in the room next door. I collapsed into bed, hoping sleep would follow, but it didn't. Instead, my mind seemed to be on duty, as though it were 8:00 a.m. on a Monday. I was thinking about every real estate deal I had in process and every possible problem that might arise.

As the hours passed, I continued to stare at the clock and count how much time I had left to sleep—if I could even fall asleep at all. This went on for what seemed like most of the night until I finally passed out from sheer exhaustion. I jolted out of bed at the first sign of daybreak, and the process started over.

When you're a workaholic, sleep is not your friend. Your mind never knows when to shut off, and your body seems to be running a marathon that you can't win.

We all know sleep is important to our health and well-being, but more than that, it's crucial to our mental health. If we're not properly rested, we cannot perform anywhere near our peak performance, and all areas of life will be affected: mental health, physical health, appearance, state of mind, and the general ability to live a happy, balanced life.

You can use the Sleep Toolbox to change your sleepless nights, and, in the process, change your life. Sleep is way too big to pass over.

Now, let's examine the Sleep Toolbox.

TOOLBOX 6:

Sleep

When you're a workaholic, your body and mind are constantly going. You may find that you do "everything" faster than the people around you. You move through life at an abnormal speed, trying to get everything done. Small talk may be annoying to you simply because it feels like a waste of time.

As the day moves into evening, you know you should slow down and switch gears from the frantic work pace, but there is no pause button. When I was operating as a workaholic, I would often get my second wind around 8:00 p.m. and work for many hours into the night. One problem with behavior like this is your brain never gets a chance to slow down or relax, and when you finally do stop, your body isn't able to relax and sleep.

Drinking alcohol and caffeine and having an irregular sleep schedule can add to the problem.

Using the Sleep Toolbox, you will reset your sleep belief system. Do you frequently hear yourself say, "I have trouble falling asleep," "I don't need very much sleep," or "I'm a night owl"?

Well, you're going to replace those beliefs with new ones.

Imagine going to bed, falling asleep quickly, sleeping soundly, waking up feeling refreshed and rested, feeling good the whole day, and not requiring that cup of coffee at 4:00 p.m. to stay alert. This is the goal we are working toward with our Sleep Toolbox. (If you have a medical condition such as insomnia, it's recommended that you check with your physician to rule out any underlying causes.)

Inside the Sleep Toolbox is something particularly important: Sleep and Relaxation Routines. By adding this to the tool-box, you agree to do all of those things every day.

Write down the list of things you're willing to do to achieve better sleep. Place this list in a folder on your computer titled 'Sleep'. Review the list you have committed to each evening. Allow fifteen minutes each day to review.

Here are some ideas to achieve better sleep:

1. **Limit your alcohol and caffeine intake.** This is a tough one, I know. I get it. If you a habit of drinking coffee throughout the day and alcohol in the evening, this will be challenging, but you can do it, and it's worth doing. Your goal should be to not drink any caffeine past noon. If you're accustomed to having coffee throughout the day, try switching to decaf coffee after noon; this trick will serve as a mind hack to curb your cravings. Start by having half caffeine and half decaf coffee to give your body time to adjust.

Don't drink any alcohol at all during the week, reserving it for the weekend. I made this one simple change, and my productivity increased 100%. I used to think one glass of wine didn't make a difference, but it does. Without it, I have more clarity and more energy to use for exercise and I sleep so much better. If you do drink alcohol on a weekday, keep it before 7:00 p.m.

2. **Stop working by 6:00 p.m.** Train your body and mind that by 6:00 p.m., you're switching gears to prepare for rest and sleep. Speak the words into existence: "I'm getting tired." "It's time to shut down for the evening." "I'll be more productive in the morning."

Turn off your computer and shut the office door. Make yourself do this. It's really difficult when you're a workaholic and are used to working day and night. But you can do it, and you must if you're going to retrain your body and mind to understand when it's time to rest and sleep. If you have a job that requires you to work at night, tailor these guidelines to your schedule. The point is to have a clear-cut "off" time when you refrain from working in order to allow plenty of time for your body and mind to relax and get enough sleep.

3. **Create a bedtime routine,** one that relaxes you. For example, you might change out of your work clothes into your pajamas and read a book in bed. Or take a bath and then put on your pajamas and listen to spa music.

   Meditation is a great way to calm both your mind and your body. Television isn't ideal because it keeps your mind active, but if you do want to watch something, choose a light movie with no violence, no news channels, please!

   You might also try a cup of caffeine-free hot tea. The important thing here is to create a routine you do every night. The routine will become a habit and help train your mind that when you perform it, your brain should switch to sleep mode.

4. **Go to bed at the same time every night.** Your body will adjust and learn when it's bedtime. This one change will make a huge difference in sleep quality.

5. **When you lay down to sleep and your mind starts racing, replace each thought with a breath.** Focus on breathing in and out slowly. This is difficult at first but will get easier. Try adding white noise; it may help take your mind off the day's events.

6. **Keep a notebook next to your bed.** If work starts to creep into your thoughts, write it down in your notebook. Getting it out of your mind will clear your thoughts, making it easier to sleep.

Over time, your body and mind will start to adjust to your bedtime routine and respond positively. I understand that making even one of these changes can be very difficult.

If you're used to working all hours of the night and going to sleep at different times, creating a routine can seem impossible, but if you use these tools in your toolbox, you will feel remarkably better. You will be implementing a self-care practice that is crucial to your health and overall well-being.

10

What Do You Like to Do in Your Free Time?
(Trick Question)

Back in the lost days, when someone would ask me this question, I would freak out. I had no idea what to say.

Free time? What the hell is that? Am I supposed to gush about all my fun and interesting hobbies?

When I was dating and still learning how to apply my toolboxes this question used to come up all the time. Honestly, it put me at a complete loss for words. I had no hobbies; not one. I spent so many years working that I didn't have any interests outside of my career.

So, I did what most workaholic single women who are trying to find their dream man do—I made up things that I hoped would make me sound interesting. I stretched the truth and said I enjoyed the outdoors and traveling, and at one point I even said I liked snowshoeing. I thought this was a good option because it would make me sound athletic—but the truth is, I hate to be cold, and when I finally did try snowshoeing, I didn't care for it.

One night, after having a couple of glasses of wine, I decided to update my dating profile. There was a hot guy on the site that I wanted to meet, and his profile listed all sorts of hobbies and interests. He was obviously athletic, and according to his profile, he was an avid skier.

Since I'm not a skier, and will never understand why anyone would sign up to freeze their ass off to slide down a mountain, I had to come up with a related hobby. Struggling to come up with one, I quickly typed *snowshoeing*…well, at least I meant to. Since it was late, and the wine had kicked in, it came out as *snow shoveling*. Without checking my text, I hit "send."

My message went something like this: *Hi, I like your profile. We seem to have some things in common, I also enjoy the outdoors and especially enjoy snow shoveling.* You can imagine my horror when I discovered my typo in the morning!

This is what happens when you're not being completely honest and you don't have any hobbies. The moral of the story is to be honest, even if it's a hard truth, and most importantly, find a hobby and discover what you like to do for fun. When you're a workaholic, it's difficult to know what you like because you're too tired, or you haven't set aside any time for fun.

So, whenever someone would ask me, "What kind of things do you like to do for fun?" there was the familiar twinge in my soul, reminding me I was not normal. Most people do have interests and hobbies, and they could answer that question with ease.

It took many years for me to discover my hobbies. I would have never known what they were if I were still a workaholic.

I discovered I love to write and have written several books. In my wildest dreams, I would have never thought I could or would write a book. I also discovered I really do love to travel. I like to see new places and love to have a trip planned at all times. I like spinning as a form of exercise and I enjoy hiking and being in nature.

None of these activities would have been possible when I was a workaholic.

If you don't have any hobbies, I urge you to find one. Just one will do for now, and then you may find that you have more just waiting to be discovered.

This is where the Hobbies Toolbox comes in:

TOOLBOX 7:

Hobbies

Maybe you already have a hobby that you enjoy, or there is something that you have always wanted to try but never had the time.

Think about that hobby. Visualize it in your mind, picture yourself doing it. You may be thinking right now that there is no way in hell that you have time for a hobby, that I just don't get it, that I don't understand how busy you really are.

Well, I *do* understand. I have been there. I spent a large part of my life with that mindset!

Try to imagine for a moment that you do have time. Erase the story you have told yourself for years. The story that tells you hobbies are for people who have free time or are retired. Remove the statement "I don't have time for hobbies" from your self-talk regimen. Replace it with, "I have time for a hobby and having a hobby will help me in multiple areas of my life. Moreover, I deserve to take personal time for myself."

The Hobby Toolbox is a place where you will set aside two hours, once a week, to focus on a chosen hobby and nothing else. That's it; only two hours once a week. There are 168 hours in a week, and you're only reserving two.

This isn't very much, but it's enough for now. The idea is to find a hobby appealing to you. You may choose two hours on a Sunday morning or a Saturday afternoon. Two hours will fly by, and if you can dedicate more time, that's great!

The rule is: you must allow two hours once a week, or you will lose the time you set aside. It will be gone forever.

Here are some ideas for hobbies that may resonate with you:

1. **Painting.** Buy a paint-by-number art kit and try it out (while sitting outside, if the weather is nice).

2. **Hiking.** Even if you just go for a walk in the park, get outside and see if nature speaks to your soul. It does to mine.

3. **Woodworking.** Make something simple with a woodworking kit.

4. **Guitar.** Take a guitar lesson (or any other musical instrument you're interested in).

5. **Read.** Sit outside with a book.

6. **Writing.** Whether it's a journal, a fiction piece, or anything else, try putting a pen to paper.

7. Skiing.

8. Snowshoeing.

9. Snow shoveling. (Just kidding...)

10. Walking. This can be very therapeutic, as well as great exercise. Crank up your music and enjoy!

11. Any other activity that speaks to your soul.

12. Make your own toolboxes, including your Memory Toolbox as part of the Twenty-Year Toolbox.

I purchased craft items from a local craft store to include eight small boxes that fit securely in a large box. I painted the boxes and named each one to correspond with the eight toolboxes you now know how to fill. I placed a bright pink padlock on the front. I brought my toolbox visualization to life. I keep it on my desk as a reminder to use each toolbox.

It's a fun craft project, give it a try!

As you get used to devoting two hours per week to your hobby, you may find you're able to relax during this time, that you can take your mind off the details of work. When the two hours are over, you may find yourself feeling better and calmer, and your mind is clearer.

The interesting thing about taking time for yourself to enjoy things—including hobbies—is that it makes you more productive in your career. I genuinely believe this.

When you're overworked, stressed, and exhausted, you're not as productive. When you're stressed, sometimes stepping away from a problem and focusing on a hobby will allow your mind to formulate a solution. You may even discover a talent that could lead to a new career!

Keep an open mind and allow your creative juices to flow.

11

Friends
(At Least, I Hope We're Still Friends...)

Sometimes I wonder how many friends other people have. I mean real friends, people with whom you have history, who have known you for many years, who know the real you. People who really get you.

For me, it's an exceedingly small group. To be exact, two. Just two people in the world whom I consider close friends. Two people who I know I can call them, and they will be there for me. They have stuck it out with me through the years—through my divorce, pregnancy, child birth, career ups and downs, and even my workaholic days.

These are the people whom I will think about when I look back at my life in my Twenty Years Toolbox. These are the people with whom I have created memories.

It's a miracle, really, that they've stuck around. You see, I wasn't a very good friend in the lost days. I never called and made time for them. If I did plan something, I would cancel. And the few times I did show up, I was not present; I was on the phone, tired, worried, or anxious, and basically a downer to be around.

Friends are one of the greatest gifts in life. We all long for companionship and to be accepted and loved. It's a basic human need.

If you're a workaholic, it's safe to say that you're not making time for your friends. How can you? You don't even make time for yourself!

In the Friends Toolbox, you're going to find the tools you need to make and nurture friendships. It's one of the most important things you can do to improve your life.

TOOLBOX 8:

Friends

Take a minute and reflect on your friends—not acquaintances but true friends. You know who they are and can probably count them on one hand. Think about the history you have together, the secrets and experiences you have shared. Imagine losing one of these people and never being able to talk or laugh with them again, never hearing their voice again.

If you're like me, you subconsciously expect your friends to always be there. It's as though I believe they will live forever, and I'll never have to say goodbye. After all, they have always been there. Logically, I know this isn't true, yet in the workaholic days, I never really stopped to acknowledge that I shouldn't take them for granted.

If you're working too much and not making time for your friends, the day will come when you wish you could go back and spend time with them, pick up the phone and talk—*really* talk—and listen to them. Your relationships are rare and important and deserve to be treated as such. In the Friends Toolbox, we are going to utilize tools to connect and stay connected with friends.

Envision a friend's name and place it in the toolbox. Visualize this person, their face, eyes, smile. Now think of a particular memory you share. Maybe it was a trip you took or a concert you attended, or maybe it was your wedding day and your friend was standing next to you as you said your vows. Anything you will always remember—place that in the toolbox, too.

Once a week, reach out to this friend. It can be an email, text, or phone call. Just a quick "Hello, thinking about you. How are you?"

At first, your friend might panic, thinking that there must be something wrong since you have probably been MIA for some time. Let them know you're trying to balance your life and miss their friendship and plan to stay in touch.

This is also a great time to apologize for your past behavior. tell them you value their friendship and would like to reconnect and stay connected. If you prefer, you can send a handwritten card to express your thoughts.

Once a month, reach out and schedule a get-together. This can be for lunch or dinner or simply to hang out. The point is, you're connecting in person once a month. When you're together, turn off your phone and be present.

The more you do this, the more you will look forward to seeing each other. Schedule two hours for these get-togethers. They're only once a month; you can do it.

If you have a friend that lives out of state or out of the country and you can't meet in person, the Friends Toolbox is also a great way to stay in touch. One of my best friends lives in Australia. We both reserve time in our Friends Toolbox to talk on the phone once a month; this keeps us connected.

Try to do this with all your friends—of which I'm betting there are only a few at most. True friends are rare. You might have to work up to include all of them, and that's okay.

If you are unable to get together in person connect by phone the important thing is to stay connected.

This may sound easy and obvious, but it's not. If it were, you would already be doing it. Putting your friends in your toolbox will be your commitment to stay connected. Someday, you will look back and be incredibly grateful that you did.

Here are some ideas for ways to connect with friends:

1. **Plan a sleepover,** order pizza or have a BBQ, watch the sunset, look at pictures of fun times you've spent together, catch up on life, and be fully present together.

2. **Go for a hike.** Nature has a way of bringing us back to earth. We are forced to slow down and quiet our minds. Have a picnic and enjoy the quiet time together.

3. **Send a gift for no reason.** Select something that is unique to your friend's personality. It could be a

bracelet, a book, a piece of clothing, or anything that speaks to you. Mail it to their home, or better yet, drop it off.

4. **Call a friend and let them know you're thinking about them.** Tell them you value their friendship and you will always be there for them. Make sure they know.

5. **Plan a kick-ass party with your closest friends!** You can also host a virtual wine tasting, Zoom happy hour, or cooking party.

A true friend is a gift and should be treasured.

The Eight Toolboxes

There they are the eight toolboxes.

If the idea of integrating them into your life seems over-whelming, let's put it in perspective. We all have the same number of hours in a day; it's up to you to decide how you want to spend those hours.

We already know that how we have chosen to spend our time thus far has not been fulfilling. We also know that material things are wonderful, but without balance in the other areas of life, ultimately, the material things aren't enough.

By applying the toolboxes in these eight categories, we are giving attention to the basic areas of our life that require attention.

We deserve to be taken care of.

We will perform better in our career when we are taking care of ourselves.

And not only will we be kicking ass in our career—we'll begin to have an awesome life!

To schedule the time allotted for each toolbox, you can use the calendar on your phone, a calendar on your desktop, a day planner, or if you enjoy crafts as one of your hobbies, you can create your own toolboxes. (See the Hobby Toolbox). Use a method that works best to protect your time. Schedule the time and to be clear on how you're using each toolbox.

The bad habits you created didn't happen overnight and changing your lifestyle won't happen overnight, either. But with each new positive habit you create, your life will improve drastically.

You're worth it; your life is waiting, and you're going to kick ass like never before!

12
Your Why

Everyone has a unique definition of success. What does it mean to you? Is it having money or status? Is it driving a certain car?

In order to be successful and sustain success, you must have a *why*. Maybe that *why* is as simple as having the financial means to buy whatever you want—a nice house, a nice car—or to be admired by your peers.

Whatever it is, identify your why and be clear about exactly what it is.

Working hard to make money is great; after all, we all know money can change your life and make things easier. But let's be clear: money alone does not bring happiness.

I know this for sure. I have known many very wealthy people who are miserable.

I mean, *really miserable*.

What money does bring is freedom. Freedom to make choices. To buy the house you want to live in, the car you want to drive, the pair of shoes you want to wear. To take the day off from work and go to your child's school play. To take a vacation you have dreamed of. To drop everything to take care of your sick parent or child.

Money brings freedom, and freedom allows choices. All your hard work has most likely led you—or will lead you—to success. Start enjoying some of that success. Reward yourself in ways that will improve your life. Spend some of your hard-earned money on something you really desire, or on a gift for someone else.

If you would like to help a family member financially, this may be your *why*.

I was able to buy a home for my mom. It was a small house, nothing to brag about, but she loved it and lived comfortably there for many years. Looking back, that house is one of the things I spent money on that brought me true joy. If you hold on tightly to money or are too tired or busy to enjoy its benefits, what's the point of having it?

Live your life and spend some of the money you have worked so hard to make.

One of my favorite pleasures in life is to buy things for the people I love without thinking about it too much. I have the freedom to do it, and it feels amazing. But my deepest *why* is to provide for my daughter.

I was a single mom for many years. I knew I had to provide for her, and I didn't want to struggle and have to worry about money. Now that she's in college, it's important for me to support her with her dream of receiving a higher education and becoming a physician. My *why* is to support her financially and emotionally to help her achieve this goal.

The more you feel your *why*, the more powerful it is, and the more success you will have.

Make a list of your dreams. What are the things you would do if you could have anything you want?

Dig deep to find your *why*. Why do you want these things? There is always a deeper reason. To simply say "I want a new Tesla because I love the way they look" isn't identifying your *why*. Think about why you want to make money and why you're working so hard.

Here are a few examples:

1. I want a new Tesla because it makes me feel successful. Driving a Tesla will remind me why I have worked hard, I will feel proud when I drive this vehicle.

The feelings of success and pride are my **why**.

2. Financial success is important to me so that I can purchase a house for my parents. They are elderly and struggling financially. I want to take the financial burden off them and so they can enjoy their life. This would bring me such joy.

This is my **why**.

3. My best friend is struggling to pay medical bills. She's working even though she's ill, I want to help relieve some of her financial pressure.

This is my **why.**

4. I desire my dream home. Living in this home will offer security and safety that I have never had in a house. This house will allow me to reward myself for my hard work and discipline. I desire and deserve this house.

This is my **why.**

5. I want to travel and see the world. There are so many places I want to visit while I'm healthy. I'm making money so I can travel where and when I want, and not have to concern myself about the money.

This is my **why**.

When you identify your *why*, you will be motivated like never before to make it happen. Spend some time and identify your Why, Write it down. *Being clear on your why is a game-changer.*

13
Dream Big...
Really Big

The sun was setting over the ocean as I sat on the deck of the bungalow in Bora Bora. I watched the clouds move in slowly, then closed my eyes. Everything felt surreal, as though I was dreaming.

This was the most beautiful place I had ever been. When I'd been planning this trip and looking at the resort online, the prices were hard to accept. It almost seemed like a typo; I had never spent that much on a hotel room. But this was not just any hotel room; this was a bungalow perched on the water with views I had only seen in movies.

After much thought and consideration, I decided to go for it. This was while I was in my post-workaholic phase, so I was enjoying vacations and using the Vacation Toolbox. I was finally enjoying the money I had worked hard to earn.

After a couple of days in paradise, I started to settle into vacation mode. I like to people-watch and am always curious what people's stories are. At dinner that evening, I observed the patrons at the restaurant on the beach. Most were couples; some were old, some were young, but all looked relaxed and happy. I couldn't help but wonder whether they had a lot of money or maxed out their credit cards to be here.

As I scanned the place, it became clear they all looked like average, normal people. Nothing jumped out at me and screamed wealth. They looked no different from people I saw every day at home.

But I have no doubt at least some of the people on that beach that night *were* different because they thought differently. They allowed themselves to dream big. Their presence in Bora Bora was proof. They knew they could have anything they wanted if they dared to dream big enough.

There is only a small percentage of people in the world who have mastered this skill. It's admirable, right? Aren't you wondering how they do it?

Quite simply, they have learned how to control their thoughts and beliefs. They have learned how to dream big.

That's it. That one skill.

Have you ever had a day when you felt like you could do anything? When you were on your game and everything fell into place? The big deal you had been working on went through, your schedule flowed on time, the parking space by the front door at the mall was available and waiting just for you.

What if every day was like that?

Dare to dream as big as you can, without limits, and it can be.

I recently completed a dream board. If you don't have a dream board, I highly recommend creating one. The purpose of the dream board is to not think logically about how you will get the things you put on the board, but rather to post whatever you "dream" about.

Pretend you can have anything you want; remember, there are no limits.

During the process of making my dream board, limiting thoughts like, "a lake house would be too expensive" entered my mind. I had to pause, and reset several times. These thoughts are limitations that need to be discarded. They curb our potential and block our dreams.

If we can eliminate the limiting beliefs in our mind, we can have the things and the life that we truly desire. Without those limiting beliefs, our subconscious mind will go to work to find a way to materialize the things we desire.

For this reason, I continue to work on dreaming big—really big—every single day.

Make a list of the things that you dream about for your future, dream **really** big. There are no limits, no one is keeping score. Maybe you want to be an actress or a bestselling author, a mother, to find your soul mate or become a millionaire.

Whatever it is...if you can dream about it, you can manifest it.

Money

Money matters—period!

I don't care what anyone says, it matters, and it matters *a lot.*

We all need money, both for basic survival (food and shelter) and well-being. The question is, what kind of relationship do you want to have with money? Do you want to struggle and resent never having enough of it? Do you want to spend your entire life working for it and not enjoying it?

Your monetary belief system determines how much you have. It's that simple. If you can change your belief system to reflect what you really want money to be for you, then it's possible.

Have you ever wondered why some people seem to be "lucky" when it comes to money? They get the breaks in life to excel faster than the rest of us. Maybe they invented something, or landed a great job right out of college, or they happened to always be in the right place at just the right time. Is it luck? Or is it something else?

It's a mindset. Yes, I will say it again, your money mindset is very powerful. Why not decide right now that you have as much money as you want, that money is flowing freely in your life? Decide you're enjoying it fully and have plenty to share with others.

There is no need to sacrifice all your time and energy to make money and have a successful career.

Why?

Because you have changed your mindset…and that will change *everything*.

There is no reason to struggle or worry about money. Just understand how you're going to "think and feel" about money.

I know there are people who say money isn't important and living a simple, non-materialistic life is more satisfying. That's great, but wouldn't it be nice to have as much money as you need and want—and then, if you choose to live a simple, non-materialistic life, you have the freedom to choose to do that? Wouldn't you prefer your lifestyle to be a choice, not a requirement?

Having as much money as you desire allows you the freedom to do the things you want and to help others in the process. Let's not pretend we don't care about money; acknowledge you like having money and that money is a positive, bright area of your life, and that is why you're going to kick ass to make more of it.

But—you're going to have a life at the same time.

Be very clear—you're not going to sacrifice your life for money, because you know you can have money *and* a balanced and healthy life. You have the tools you need to nurture both your personal finances and self-care. Even if you've had a less-than-ideal relationship with money in the past, you have the ability to change that.

I am a strong believer in affirmations. I read mine out loud every morning while I enjoy my coffee. By starting each morning this way, I'm better positioned to approach each day with a positive mindset.

I don't watch television, listen to music, or check the news until I have set my mind to my intentions. Try adding these affirmations to your daily thoughts (or make up some of your own that resonate with you).

- Money is flowing freely in my life. I have as much as I need or want.

- I am free to spend money on things that make me happy because I have plenty.

- I have enough time and money to take care of my body, mind, and spirit.

- I am financially secure.

- I am healthy in body, mind, and spirit.

- I love my career because it allows freedom and financial security.

- I make money easily and have plenty of free time to fully enjoy my life.

15
Not My Cup of Tea

Every morning at 4:00 a.m., my mom would leave for work. She was the breadwinner in the family. As she settled into her old Dodge with the ripped front seat, she glanced at her watch and stepped on the gas; she couldn't be late to her job at the factory. This was the best job she had ever had. It allowed her to support me and my two siblings.

My father was self-employed, and he could never be counted on to contribute financially, so Mom had to bring in a steady income. We had a house, but there wasn't much spending money. We lived paycheck to paycheck. This became a way of life that everyone in my family seemed to accept.

When I was in the sixth grade, I walked in the door after school, tossed my backpack on the kitchen table, and to my surprise, saw that Mom was home. She was never home during the day.

"Hi Mom, what are you doing here? Did you get off early?" I was happy to see her; she worked so much that any time with her made me happy. That's when I noticed she had been crying. Her eyes were red, and she looked away, not making eye contact and not saying anything, as though she was afraid to speak. "Mom, are you okay?"

Finally forcing the words out, she spoke softly, looking at the floor. "I got laid off from work."

An eleven-year-old doesn't fully understand what "laid off" means, but I knew it had to do with Mom's job, and, from the look on her face, it was not good news.

For the next few months, Mom was home every day. She looked and acted like a different person. She was sad and seemed to be crying all the time. Money was even tighter than before, and the days between our usual trips to the grocery store seemed to stretch out even longer. There wasn't much food in the house, and I no longer had my daily lunch money. It was impossible to ignore the fact that we needed money and food.

One afternoon, I came home from school to find Mom putting away groceries. There was so much food, the kitchen table was overflowing with bags. Mom quietly put away the groceries, but I couldn't hide my excitement.

"Wow, you got cookies…and cereal!" I continued to rummage through the bags. Mom remained silent. "Where did all this food come from?"

Finally, she looked up. "I had to get food stamps to get us groceries." She was fighting back the tears.

I had no idea what that meant, but I did know Mom was upset about it. "What does that mean?" I asked, almost afraid to hear the answer.

Mom looked up slowly meeting my stare. "It's money from the government to help us because we can't help ourselves."

The words punctured my soul like a jagged knife. The sharp edges tore my skin and lodged deep in the crevices. It was the kind of pain that settles in to stay.

In that exact moment, I knew I would find a way to support myself. I would never depend on anyone for money. I would never need money because I would have plenty of my own. Struggling would never be my style!

That moment changed me forever, but I'm grateful for it, because it taught me so much about myself and changed my life's course.

We all come from different backgrounds. Some of us come from privileged families, some don't. Either way, our childhoods played a role in who we are today. But regardless of your past—whether it was good, bad, or somewhere in the middle—at the end of the day, it's up to you to decide how your future will look.

Some people choose to follow in the footsteps of their family and repeat the cycle. If your family was poor, you can choose to accept that you will be poor, too. It's a choice, not a requirement. I admire successful people who have come from a difficult or poor childhood, because I know they rose above the challenges of their upbringing, and worked hard for what they have.

I love a good underdog story, someone that has made their own way and succeeded against all odds. To me, that is true success!

If you're a workaholic, it's possible that you're working too much due to a fear that you won't have enough. You believe on a subconscious level you have to work all the time in order to ensure a secure future. This is a belief coming from scarcity instead of abundance.

The problem with this belief is either you can't enjoy the money you make or that you believe you can never have enough. Take time to understand how your childhood is affecting your work habits.

Do you think you have to work this hard because you fear running out of money?

Do you feel you have to make more and more money, regardless of how much you make?

Do you feel guilty if you make too much money?

Do you feel worthy of the money you make?

Maybe you're overworking to avoid other problems.

After about five years of marriage to my first husband, I knew I was with the wrong person. We were not compatible at all, we had very little in common, and our views about money were polar opposite. He is a good person and a good father to our daughter, but we should have never gotten married.

Rather than deal with this huge problem in my life, I worked all the time. This was my way of avoiding something I didn't know how to deal with—it was easier to work, to hide from my problem.

Give this some thought. It's very personal for each of us.

After you understand *why* you're a workaholic, it's easier to put a stop to the dysfunctional behavior.

16
Gold Card

Imagine for a moment you can have anything you want in life. What comes to mind? Is it a certain house or car? Maybe it's a million dollars? Or maybe you want to be a size three with no cellulite and a flat stomach.

When I was a workaholic, I always wanted more, more, more of everything.

There were many material things I wanted, and since I'm in the real estate business and see houses on a regular basis, I always wanted a bigger and better house. I also wanted new and better furniture. If I was showing a house and saw a beautiful couch, suddenly my couch wasn't good enough.

The same was true for my car. I always wanted the newest and best model. I was also very critical of my clothing; I would shop online since I didn't make time to actually go to a clothing store. I would buy expensive clothes and most of the time I would not wear them nor return them. I was, of course, in my mind, too busy to go to the post office and return them.

Purchasing the clothes made me feel better in the moment, even though I never actually wore them. This went on for years. I was always chasing something to fill the void of not having enough, not being enough.

The reality is, I would never have enough, because I was wishing for the wrong things. None of these things would make me happy. If you find yourself buying things, yet unsatisfied and always wanting more, take a step back, put your gold card down, and think about what the hell is actually going on inside your mind and your wallet.

Recently, I was experiencing some health issues related to menopause and I went to the doctor. My regular OBGYN was not available, but I had to get in and see someone immediately, so I was given an appointment with a different doctor.

He was a laid-back, likable guy who seemed knowledgeable. He ordered some blood tests and suggested a minor procedure. I left there feeling better.

A couple of days passed; I was happily singing in my car, driving to meet with a long-term real estate client when my phone rang. I answered without thinking. It was Dr. G. He sounded stressed and not at all like the relaxed guy I met in the office a few days ago.

He proceeded to explain my blood tests came back and my CA125 level was very high. He told me I needed to see a specialist as soon as possible.

Then he said, "I think you have ovarian cancer."

The words felt like sharp glass, shattering, then cutting my skin until it bled. I was still driving and trying to focus. I managed to get the specialist's name and hung up.

I pulled over and tried to comprehend what just happened.

The very first words that came to mind were "I might be out of time."

The second thought I had was, "I wasted so much time."

When I called to make the appointment with the oncologist, it was as though they were waiting for my call, and they asked me to come in the next day. I had never heard of an oncologist and didn't even know what they did, so I googled it. There was that word again: *cancer*.

The surgeon recommended a hysterectomy. Surgery was scheduled for two weeks from then. He said that he would not know if I had cancer until he opened me up and they tested the tissue.

It was the hardest and longest two weeks of my life. The fear was overwhelming.

What if I have cancer? What if I die? What if I'm out of time?

The questions tumbled and tripped over themselves in my mind. I prayed, mediated, and practiced affirmations every day, all day. The thoughts wouldn't go away.

What if I don't have any more time with my daughter and never get to meet my grandchildren? What if I can't spend any more time with my husband?

Never once did I say to myself, *I wish I would have gotten that new Tesla or a bigger house.* Material things were the farthest thing from my mind.

At the end of our life, the things that matter are the memories that we created and the time we spent with our loved ones. The other things that seemed so important for so many years are not the things that really matter at the end of our life.

Isn't it ironic that we spend most of our life chasing financial success to buy material things that, at the end of our life, really aren't the most important things? Understanding this before it happens can be life-changing.

The surgery went well, and I didn't have cancer. My prayers were answered!

Bursting with gratitude and a new appreciation for life, I knew then (just as I know now) that I have been given another chance to live right **now.**

I have a new appreciation for my body and am so grateful that my body had the strength to make it through the surgery and to give me another chance to live! I will never say another bad word about my body again, ever. I realize now how shallow those negative thoughts and words were. My body may not be perfect, I'm not at my goal weight, my cute beige shorts don't fit me, my stomach isn't flat, and I have cellulite, BUT…I love my body. I have a strong kick-ass body!

When you're buying things, ask yourself why you're buying them. Is it because you really want them and deserve them—or are you buying them to feel better about yourself?

I'm not suggesting that you shouldn't have nice things. I'm ALL about having nice things that you really want and that will elevate your life. You work hard and you should reward yourself, but there is a difference between purchasing something to fill a void and purchasing things to reward yourself.

Happiness cannot be found in material possessions alone.

Keep this in mind when you make a purchase and understand the "why" before you sign the next check.

Stay focused on your eight toolboxes. Allow time for the areas of your life that are important for a healthy balanced life.

Remember, at the end of your life, the things that matter won't be found on your gold card statement.

17
Let Freedom Ring

When you hear the word *freedom*, what comes to mind? What does it mean to you?

Do you think about money?

Freedom and money go hand in hand. Money affords you the freedom to do the things that are important to you and to enjoy the experiences to create kick-ass memories.

If you want to be a stay-at-home parent and be with your child, you need to have enough money to allow yourself the freedom to do this. If you want to see the world and travel, it's going to be a hell of a lot easier to see and enjoy it if you have money.

Freedom allows you to do whatever you want, and money is the vehicle to get you there. The question is, how much money do you really need to live the life you want, to have the freedom you desire?

In my workaholic days, I had no idea how much money I really "needed." I just knew I wanted to make lots of it. In the process of making money, I became addicted to the feeling money gave me. Regardless of how much money I made, I always needed more.

I was similar to an alcoholic who starts out drinking a beer every now and then—the next thing they know, they're drinking a twelve-pack a day. I needed more and more. I never stopped to quantify how much money I needed to do the things I wanted to, or what my *why* was.

As I worked my way up in the real estate world and began to sell more and more houses, I also started to sell higher-priced houses. At the height of my workaholic days, I worked with a buyer who wanted to purchase a high-end condominium. Price was not an issue.

After shopping for several months, I had a contract secured for $2.5 million dollars on a gorgeous brand-new condo with a spectacular view. The commission on this property would be my largest yet: $70,000. I was so excited; with this commission check, I could relax and not be pressured to work all the time. This would be more money than I ever had at one time.

As I got closer to the closing day, I became more and more nervous and excited. This was really happening! This was going to change *everything!*

The closing took place and went smoothly. In fact, it was one of the easiest real estate transactions of my career. After the closing, I walked to my Lexus, holding the check in my hand. I settled into the front seat and tossed the white envelope on the passenger's seat. This was the check that would change everything, the amount of money that would simplify my life. I would finally have "enough."

I slowly reached over and re-read the amount. $70,000. It was real. It was mine.

The first thought that came to my mind? "That's not *that* much money," followed by "I can make *more*." My emotions numb, I drove out of the parking lot. The early excitement had dulled, overshadowed by my desire for more.

Deep down inside, I knew this was not normal.

I brushed that thought aside and hurried back to work.

Part of my issue was not having clear goals, knowing my *why*, and the understanding of how much money I actually needed to accomplish those goals. If I had had that clarity, the $70,000 would have meant something. I would have had a greater emotional reaction and appreciation to that victory.

Making money just to make money, with no clarity as to why and how much you need to reach your goals, will lead to the negative cycle of no amount ever being enough. It won't lead to freedom, nor happiness.

Decide what freedom means to you and how much money you need to achieve it. Having clarity is powerful!

18

Goals

Let's talk about goals.

We all know goals are important, and we should have them, but let's think about *why* we need them. When we set important goals for ourselves, we feel it. That's right, *feel* it, not just think about it or write it down on our list of things we think we should write down.

I'm talking about something completely different.

If you can define something really important to you, something you would do anything to have, that you can't live without, something that will change and elevate your life, then you can call it a goal.

You may already have a list of goals; a list that you've had for years. These goals are stale and need to be updated with ones you can *feel*.

Let me give you an example of what I mean. Below is a list of goals you may think are goals, but you don't really *feel* them or want them bad enough to actually accomplish them.

• Exercise and lose weight

• Work less

• Start dating

The problem with these so-called "goals" is there is no clarity or feeling behind them.

Let's try a different approach to identifying and writing down our goals. Below are some examples you can personalize for your own life.

• **Goal:** I want to exercise and lose weight.

• **Revised Goal:** I will lose twenty pounds by the end of November. I will lose two pounds per week by following a healthy eating plan and exercising five days a week, 8:00 – 8:30 a.m. I want to lose this weight and be comfortable in my own skin. I miss the days when I felt pretty and good about myself.

I'm willing to let go of the mindless eating and skipping workouts just because I'm not in the mood, and would rather spend all my time working. I'm willing to make these changes so I can feel good and be healthy again.

I will place thirty minutes per day in my exercise toolbox. I will start today. Not tomorrow. Today.

- **Goal:** I want to work less.

- **Revised goal:** Today I have made the decision to work less.

I will have a balanced life. I admit I have a problem with overworking and it's sabotaging my life and relationships. My relationship with my family is the most important thing to me in the world, and I never make time for them.

I will use my two hours a day in my Time Toolbox to spend quality time with my family starting today. Not tomorrow. Today.

- **Goal:** I want to start dating.

- **Revised goal:** I have made the conscious decision I'm ready to meet someone and have a healthy relationship.

I know I'm afraid due to the failure of my last relationship. I was hurt and don't want to be hurt again. I'm willing to risk getting hurt again to find love.

I don't want to grow old alone, while longing for a true companion. I will join a social group and research dating sites. If I find a dating web site that I'm comfortable with, I will join on a trial period. I will keep an open mind and be open to meeting new people.

I will implement my Time Toolbox to focus on activities and places I can go to meet someone new. I will start today. Not tomorrow. Today.

Notice the difference in how we are describing our goals versus simply identifying what they are. List them with honesty and feeling. Be honest about why you want these things and how you will achieve them. In order to maximize our goals, we need to *feel* our goals.

When you set goals at work, they follow a specific formula, there's even a formula: SMART (specific, measurable, attainable, relevant, time-based). Applying this formula to your personal goals has the same positive affect.

Try it. Write down your goals, including the details of how you will feel once they are achieved and how you feel now—the more detail, the better. This is personal and not to be shared with anyone else, so feel safe being honest with yourself. There is no right or wrong goal, as everyone is different.

One person's goal may be to run a 10k marathon, while another may have the goal to walk around the block. Any goal you genuinely want to achieve, and that you can feel, is a good goal and worthy of being written down.

Resist judgment of where you are today. The fact is, you're here, and you're working on yourself to be a better, healthier person, and that matters. Be kind to yourself and know you can achieve any goal that you truly desire, feel, and set your mind to achieving.

As to what you aspire toward—don't concern yourself with what others may think. Any goal you truly desire to accomplish should be pursued with passion.

19
Dreams, Dreams, and More Dreams

Having goals and dreams go hand in hand.

I know we have already touched on dreaming big, but let's explore that concept deeper.

When you hear the term *dream big*, what comes to mind? A mansion or a Ferrari, maybe? Imagine your life being exactly what you want it to be—what would that look like? When I was new to the real estate world, I didn't know what my dreams were. I just knew that I wanted to make a lot of money.

Early in my career, I had a new client who wanted to purchase several investment properties. He was very wealthy and lived in an area of town I had heard of but had never visited. The first real estate deal we completed together changed my life, not because I made a lot of money from it, but because I got a glimpse into his world. After I prepared the purchase contract, he suggested I bring it to his home so he and his wife could sign.

I entered his address into my GPS. As I drove through the neighborhood, I could sense the environment changing. Just by driving down the street, I could sense how different life was for the people who lived there.

I slowed down as I approached the address. A large, gated entrance set the precedent for the property I was about to see. As the gate slowly opened, I felt my heart skip a beat. It was difficult not to gasp at my surroundings. I had never seen a home of this caliber.

Walking inside the house, I smiled and tried not to stare as I caught a glimpse of the outdoor pool, cabana, and pool house. In my head, I imagined what it would be like to live there.

Quite literally, this experience changed my life.

Driving out of the neighborhood, I carefully observed the homes around me and subconsciously selected the one I liked best. I can still see it my mind after all these years: a Tuscan-style home resembling a castle, painted a light gray color with burgundy shutters, a striking waterfall adorning the entryway of the long circular driveway, large planters with beautiful flowers sitting proudly on each side of the front door. I imagined soft jazz music playing inside, welcoming me home after a day at work.

Since then, I have been in and sold many high-end homes, but this one is still clear as day in my mind. Why? Because living in a home like that became my dream. I dreamed big— really big—on that day so many years ago, and that dream never left me.

Dreaming big needs to be specific; it can be a dream about anything you want, but it must be specific. There is no dream that is too big. After all, it's a dream, right? What is the purpose of dreaming if we limit ourselves?

Whatever your dream is, believe in it, don't let anybody kill it, and guard it with your life. Hold it tightly and only share it with people you trust and who also believe in dreaming big.

Complete your dream board and keep it somewhere highly visible, where you'll see it daily. I keep mine in my office. I see and feel the presence of my dream board every day.

Dreaming is fun, it feels good, and it can change your life. Start dreaming and make sure it's for something you want so bad, you can see it and sense it. Remember that there are no limits. Don't concern yourself with how or the how much. Just dream. The bigger the better!

Remove the limitations in your mind so your subconscious can get to work in finding a way to bring those dreams to life.

Become crystal clear on your dreams so you can manifest them into reality.

20
Words

Words matter. We use words every day without thinking about them. We take them for granted and speak without forethought. I'm here to tell you—we have to watch our words! The words we choose can impact our life negatively or positively.

Think about the people you spend time with on a daily basis, the people you work with and live with. Are there some people you enjoy talking to because they always seem to have something interesting to say? Or because they are positive and seem to find the bright side of situations, even when there is a big problem? Or because they are calm and have a way of making everyone feel better even in the midst of chaos?

On the flip side, are there some who never stop talking and never really say anything? Some whom you avoid when their name appears on caller ID, and hope they will settle for leaving a message? Some who are total downers?

Let's face it—the words you use and the energy you emit define who you are.

Be careful with your words. It's easy to be negative if you're having a bad day; after all, we are human, and we are going to have some bad days.

If you catch yourself speaking negatively, just stop and replace those words. Say out loud, "That's not what I meant to say," and rework your thought. If you catch yourself gossiping, stop and change your words.

If you're angry and start saying—or even worse, screaming—things you don't mean, pause, breathe, and change your words. We aren't perfect, but we can be aware of and change our words. Understanding the power of our words is important.

Avoid talking to fill in space. It's okay to be silent. There are times when silence is exactly what is appropriate. Consider the times when you have been with a friend or a significant other and you were both silent and it felt completely comfortable. Isn't that a wonderful feeling?

Use your words to uplift someone, to brighten their day. By simply using kind words, and not being critical or speaking just for the sake of talking, your words can bring positive changes to both your mood and someone else's.

Think before you speak. I know this is easier said than done. Just being aware is half the battle. If there is one thing I have learned in my real estate business, it's to think before I speak.

In negotiations, the person who talks most is typically the person who is losing.

Our words matter.

Watch your words as though your life depends on it...because it does.

21

Are You Holding Onto an Old Pair of Shoes?

Have you ever taken stock of the people you are surrounded with and asked yourself if you are compatible? As we get older, we all get more set in our ways. Envision the people who make up your life: your friends, your family, your spouse or significant other, your coworkers, your boss. The way you interact with these people speaks volumes.

Have you ever been around a married couple who bicker constantly and never seem to get along? I have always wondered how anyone could be in a relationship like that. How about the couple who has been married for twenty years and still seem to be madly in love—how do they do it? Did they just get lucky and find their soulmate?

Be careful who you allow into your circle of friends. Make sure they are aligned with the life you're working so hard to create. The truth of the matter is that some people just don't fit into your life. They could have at one time, but now you and this other person are totally different people. It's not that they're bad people—in fact, they might be great—they're just not great for *you*.

Maybe you have that one friend whom you know you have grown apart from, but they are familiar, and you have a history, so you hang on to the friendship even though it does not serve either one of you anymore. Or maybe you're in a relationship with someone who does not treat you with respect. You know you deserve better, but you care about them and don't want to let go, so you keep holding on, hoping they will change. Or maybe there is someone in your life who is negative, always talking about the bad things in life, gossiping about other people, and complaining, and when you're around them you find yourself complaining, too.

Evaluate the people you associate with and ask yourself if the relationship adds to your life. If not, it may be time to move on. Be honest with yourself, you know who needs to go and who should stay. Just because it's familiar doesn't mean you should keep it.

Let me give you an example. Picture a favorite pair of shoes. At first you love them, you wear them with everything, they are comfortable, you can walk in them all day without your feet hurting, they look cute and make you feel smart and stylish.

Over time, they get scuffed up, so you polish them, and then they look good again. More time passes, your style changes, the shoes don't really fit with the rest of your wardrobe anymore, but you hang onto them. You move several times over the years and always pack your favorite shoes, tossing them in the back of the closet but never wearing them anymore.

Years later, you take them out and consider wearing them. You notice the heel is broken on the right side, but you try them on and look in your full-length mirror. They look odd, like they belong to someone else, and aren't your style at all; in fact, you would be embarrassed to wear them anywhere. You finally toss them in the trash and realize you have been holding on to this pair of shoes way too long. Now you have room in your closet for a new pair of shoes, ones that reflects who you are today.

Relationships can be the same. Look at your relationship and ask yourself, "Have I outgrown this?"

Surround yourself with people whom you admire and who lift you up. Let go of the relationships that don't work for you anymore. You're way too busy to share your time with those people.

Now that you're using your Friends Toolbox wisely, you can be very selective about who you want to share your time with. You're making positive changes in every area of your life, and this area cannot be ignored—it's too big and too important to ignore.

It's time to clear out the old to make room for the new!

Have you ever noticed how good you feel when you clean out your closet? I'm talking about decluttering—going through all your old clothes and getting rid of any that you haven't worn in years or that don't represent the person that you are today. As you clear out the closet, you're making room for new clothes, new experiences. It feels great because subconsciously you know these old clothes were taking up room in your closet and in your life.

This is the same thing that we are doing in relationships that we have outgrown. It may be hard at first, but with each step forward and each toss of something outdated that you no longer need, you will know that you have cleared the way for something better—something that reflects who you are and your life *now*.

22
The Super Hero

Since we are on the subject of getting rid of the things that no longer serve us, it's time to ditch the negativity in your life.

Negativity affects us all; it goes with the territory of living and being human. Negative thoughts words and behaviors may be coming from your coworkers, family, friends, and even from yourself. Negative thoughts and words may be sabotaging you in ways you don't even realize.

If you desire something in your life and find yourself thinking of all the reasons you can't have it, or why it won't work, the negative energy you're sending to this area of your life is blocking all possibilities of what you want. You're creating a self-fulfilling prophecy, and *not* the one you want.

Our thoughts are a powerful energy force that is very obedient, so it's important to control our thoughts. Why do we allow negativity to control our life? Because we are conditioned to think and talk this way, we have formed a habit that we need to break. The desire to do more and have more can sabotage our success and steal our happiness. The desire to be perfect—to be a super hero—adds to our negative thought process.

Perform an experiment this week: pay attention to the conversations happening around you and in your own head. You may hear things like: "it's always something," "life is hard," "I'm so tired," "traffic sucks," "my job is hard," "I screwed up!" and on and on…

These are the thoughts and words that are sabotaging the good things waiting for you on the other side of negativity. The other side of negativity is the "bright side;" this is the side we want to be on.

In your experiment, every time you think, hear, or say a negative comment, replace it with a positive thought. If you hear yourself say "traffic sucks," replace it with "I'll be out of traffic soon and I have had a productive day" you will notice your energy change instantly.

Negativity and a super-hero complex are best friends. They love to cause havoc! The super hero is a perfectionist. If you have cast yourself in the starring role as the super hero, it's time for an immediate shift.

You need to recast yourself into a role you love, one that inspires you.

To a perfectionist, everything is a huge deal. They manufacture stress for themselves and everyone around them. When we play the perfectionist/super-hero role, we expect way too much out of ourselves and then when we don't make the cut, we denigrate ourselves and allow negativity to take over.

This does not serve us well—and does not fit in our life anymore! The perfectionist super hero is a pain in the ass that really deserves an eviction notice, and you're just the one to hand it out!

Would you expect a close friend to be perfect? If they aren't, would you criticize them? I don't think so. Yet, we set outrageous expectations for ourselves, then feel bad when we can't check off all the boxes on our to-do list, even though Clark Kent would fall short.

The super hero is relentless and always wants more.

So, what if you got up at 5:00 a.m. and packed a delicious healthy lunch for your daughter's school field trip and even included an encouraging note, you forgot to add one of the cookies you made last night especially for the field trip—so now the super hero reminds you all day that you are a terrible mom and won't ever get it right.

Decide right now you're done with this negative, over-achieving, energy-sucking critic. Decide to kick some ass and set a new boundary; negativity is banned from your life. You have no room for it anymore!

When I finally decided to kick negativity's ass and dropped my super-hero cape, I applied a new habit: when I have a negative thought, I change the thought to a positive one, and think to myself, or say out loud "bye, critic." I'm reminding myself we don't hang out with the negative super hero—she's an outdated bad habit who is no longer invited.

Imagine you just moved into a new house. This is your dream home you have worked for and manifested into your life. This house represents you and the person you want to be. It's immaculate and beautifully decorated, and it reflects your kick-ass life.

Now, imagine a group of old college friends you used to party with. Uninvited, they show up at your door to party and catch up. They are drinking and smoking, and want to stay up all night partying. You have nothing in common with them, they are loud and chugging beer and you're uncomfortable when you must request that they do not smoke in your house.

You know that you have outgrown this group of friends; they represent a mindset you don't relate to anymore. You have worked hard on your growth and now you have to move on. You wish them well, and hold on to the good memories while honoring your truth today.

You have to be strong enough to kick ass and let go of the old habits in order to live in the now.

Is it difficult? Yes!

Is it worth it? Absolutely!

Don't be confused by old habits. Just because they are familiar doesn't mean they have a place in your mind or in your life.

Become a total badass in this area of your life. Be very clear you're only allowing positive thoughts in your mind and be selective about the people you surround yourself with.

Will bad things happen? Yes, they will—we live in a dysfunctional world and all kinds of negative things will happen, but you can choose to approach those things with positive thoughts. Even in the most difficult times, keeping this frame of mind will make the hardest times easier.

Toss your super hero cape out!

Better yet, trade it in for a kick-ass outfit you love!

23
Positive Believing

Do you live your life believing things will go your way? Or do you expect the worst to happen at any given time?

This, my friend, is a question you need to answer.

Your beliefs affect everything, and I do mean *everything*. I know you've heard of positive thinking, and that's great, but I'm talking about something different—I'm talking about *positive believing*. The art of believing that everything is aligned to go your way in life.

Now, I know what you're thinking right now—life isn't a fairy tale, and everything doesn't go perfectly all the time. Agreed…but what if you believed it did and it will?

If you change your mindset to believe all good, all the time, your subconscious mind will go to work immediately to make that happen. Your subconscious will *believe* you. Then, when life doesn't go as planned, your subconscious will still believe things will go your way and turn out well, therefore proactively reacting in a positive way.

We can't control everything in life, and bad things can and will happen, but when we change our thoughts to trust in positive outcomes, every situation has a much higher chance of going well. This isn't easy; we have been thinking a certain way our entire life. But our old way of thinking does not serve us well anymore. Replacing those thoughts with this new belief system will change everything we do.

Start today by simply replacing every negative thought with a positive one.

Here is an example: "I have such a busy day. I'm going to run out of time. I'm so stressed out." The new thought: "Today is a good day. I have enough time to get everything done that I need to do."

Now, here's the important part: *Believe it.*

Don't just say it, *believe it.*

In your mind, decide that it's done.

Start implementing this habit into your everyday life, and I mean apply it to every situation. Every time you have a negative thought, change it immediately.

By doing this, you're reprograming your belief system. Negative thoughts have absolutely no benefit and no longer fit in your life. They have to go!

This one action can completely transform your life for the better.

24

Faith

Since we're on the subject of believing, let's talk about faith.

When you hear the word, *faith*, what comes to mind? Do you think of religion or a church? Let us set religion aside for a second and think about the word *faith* and what it means.

The definition of faith in *dictonary.com* is as follows: Confidence or trust in a person or thing.

My favorite definition of faith is as follows: faith is believing in something you cannot see.

In our lives, there are lots of things we cannot see, but we know they are real. For example, you know blood is flowing through your veins right now, though you cannot see it, but you have faith that it's flowing where it needs to flow in order to keep you alive. The truth is you already have faith in all kinds of things.

Why not have faith in something you consciously choose and want in your life?

Having faith is believing the things you dream about—success, health, love, etc.—are going to work out. If you can believe your heart will continue to function, your car is going to start, your spouse isn't going to cheat on you, and many other things, you can and should have faith in yourself and your dreams!

Religion is personal; we all have our own beliefs. There aren't any right or wrong answers. Religion is an area fueled with emotion, just the word "religion" affects some people in a negative way.

For some people, it's a "trigger" that can lead back to childhood. Maybe your parents made you go to church every Sunday, and you resented the fact that you had to be there. Perhaps you grew up in a strict religious family, and as soon as you could, you rebelled and got as far from religion as possible. Or maybe you're deeply religious, and your religious faith is a big part of your life.

Wherever you land, this is personal to you. Include faith as part of your journey through life because, without it; you're missing out and cheating yourself of a fantastic gift, free for the taking.

I cannot imagine not having faith. I pray every day for almost everything; sometimes I wonder if God is getting tired of hearing from me.

Here is the great thing about praying and having faith that things will work out—you can *let it go.* Yes, you can turn it over and move on. Believing there is something bigger and more powerful than you can relieve a lot of stress. If you're the one who has to take care of everything, fix everything, and have all the answers…that, my friend, is a lot of pressure.

I pray for health, clarity, wisdom, my family's health. I pray for every real estate deal to be in the best interest of my client and for them to be in the home that will make them happy. I pray for the correct words to write on this page.

I pray to heal when I'm ill, for my loved ones to be healthy and I pray for the blemish on my chin to go away before my next big event. Seriously, my friends, I pray for everything! And then, I have faith and *let go.*

God has bailed me out of so many situations I cannot even count them; my prayers have been answered so many times, it's mind-boggling. I feel blessed in knowing and having faith that God is there listening and taking care of all the stress here on earth. This allows me to focus on my life and my joy, not all the negative worrisome things in life.

Whether you go to church every Sunday or you have never stepped foot in a church, I'm asking you to believe in something bigger than yourself. If that isn't God for you, then maybe it's the universe or a higher power. Have faith things will work out for the best.

Will things go wrong? Yes!

Life isn't a box of chocolates but when we have faith that things will work out—even when they aren't as we hoped—if we hold on to our faith, I believe all things work out as they are meant to. The thought of going through life without faith is almost unbearable to me.

We are all on our own path in life. Many of my friends don't share my same Christian beliefs, including my best friend of forty-three years I know it's not my place to try to change her beliefs. Instead, I accept her and she accepts me exactly as I am.

Though we don't agree on religion, we do agree that Faith rocks!

Faith is more significant than just *thinking* positive; faith is *believing*. There is a big difference here; it's easy to say, "I'm going to think positive." Faith is praying and trusting that everything is on track and will work out. The conclusion may not be as you hoped, but please dare to believe it will be as it should be and then let it go.

We should have grace for each other regardless of where we are on the path of life and where we stand in our beliefs. Some of us may detour and change our faith, some of us may find God when we least expect it, and for some of us, the path will never include an organized religion.

Regardless of where you stand, find the courage to allow faith into your life. Ask for help and clarity when needed and believe the greater good is in process.

Faith is an important key to having an exceptional life!

25
Your Body is the Boss

If I were to ask you what the most important thing in the world is to you, what would your answer be? Would your health make the list? It would make mine.

Think about it for a second. If we don't have our health, our life will be challenging and reaching our goals will become secondary to our health.

Our bodies will tell us what we need if we listen.

For example, if you're tired, stop working and rest. That sounds laughably simple, but often that isn't what we do. Instead, we drink caffeine and push our bodies to keep going. When we abuse our body with the wrong food, too much alcohol, no exercise, not enough rest, and so on, our body is unable to function at full capacity.

Over time, this can take a toll. I know you've heard all this before, but maybe you never really listened. Maybe you're ready to make a change, to listen to your body.

Be kind to your body. Treat it like a precious gem. Eat healthy foods, rest, treat yourself to a massage on a regular basis, and exercise. If this sounds unrealistic and you're thinking, "Yeah, right, in a perfect world. I don't have time for any of that," think about what would happen if you got ill, *really* ill.

You would *have* to focus on your health. The truth is you do have time and your health, and your life depends on it.

Schedule a monthly massage, facial, or pedicure. Prioritize this appointment just like all the other appointments on your calendar. Take time alone to recharge.

You might like to rent a private cabin or a beach house by yourself for a weekend where you can read and rest and rejuvenate. Does this sound elaborate or selfish? Self-care isn't selfish or elaborate at all. Its purpose is simply to train our subconscious that we *matter*, that we are as important as everyone and everything else in our world.

When we practice self-care, we can give freely to the people we love, and we can work at peak performance, therefore making more money for ourselves and our family's future. We can function from a place of abundance, not scarcity.

Your body is the boss. You can decide to accept this and treat your body with respect and love, and your body will respond in kind; or you can abuse your body until it finally decides enough is enough and turns on you.

Caring for your body is one of the most rewarding things you can do for yourself, and it is an absolute requirement for a kick-ass life.

26

Time to Start Kicking Some Serious Ass

We have covered a lot of ground so far on fostering the different aspects of a balanced, kick-ass life. You're still here, and that tells me you're serious about making these changes. Your amazing life is waiting, so let's keep going!

I introduced eight toolboxes that are equipped with the tools we need to drastically improve eight crucial areas of our lives. Let's take another look at our toolboxes.

1. Time

2. Sex

3. Plan and Take a Vacation

4. Twenty Years

5. Exercise

6. Sleep

7. Hobbies

8. Friends

I would recommend starting with Toolbox 1 and implementing those tools into your daily life before moving to Toolbox 2, and so on.

If you try to focus simultaneously on all eight toolboxes, you may get overwhelmed and lose focus.

After the tools in Toolbox 1 have become a part of your daily routine, you're ready to move to Toolbox 2. For some of you, this may only take a few days; for others it may take several months.

Work at your own pace. Each toolbox contains powerful life changes. Implementing just one will make a dramatic difference in your life.

Now that we have the tools and the big picture to create the life we desire; the time has come for us to zero in on the fine print. We're going to laser-focus on the core pieces of our life and decide exactly how to improve on them.

Putting all the pieces together will create the life of our dreams, a truly kick-ass life.

This is the fun part!

Make a list of all the important areas of your new, kick-ass life. Elaborate on each piece—the more detail you provide, the better.

Your Home

Write down the details of the home where you want to live. If you have a certain one in mind, print a photo of it and post it on your dream board. Write down all the specs.

Where is it located? How many square feet is it? What color is the exterior? How many bedrooms and bathrooms? What does the backyard look like? The more specific you are, the better. This is your dream home!

Maybe your dream home is a small beach house, or a cabin in the mountains, or a mansion perched over the coast. Look online at different styles of homes to determine what resonates with you.

If you're already living in your dream home, congratulations —you created it and made it happen! Regardless of whether you already live in your dream home, know that you can choose it and it is meant for you alone!

Have fun visualizing this house and imagining how you will feel when you're there. Imagine how you will decorate it. Remember, your home should be the place where you can retreat from the world and find peace and rest—a place that is soothing to your soul, and a place you can be proud to call home.

This doesn't mean it has to be a mansion; it can be a small place you have remodeled to make it your home. The paint colors and furnishings should speak to you. Have you ever walked into someone's house and the warmth engulfs you, radiating from all sides?

I love houses like that because you just know the people who live there love it. It reflects who they are. Strive to create a home like this for yourself. Your home should be your safe space, the place you love to be.

One of my dreams is to own a beach house. I have pictures of my dream beach house on my dream board. I have spent days and weeks online looking at furniture to decorate each room. I've picked out paint colors and the rocking chairs that will sit on the front porch.

I have no idea where my beach house is. In fact, I haven't even nailed down the state yet, but I know exactly what it looks like and can feel myself living there for part of the year.

I have no idea how much it costs or how I'm going to afford it. That's okay, because I have identified the beach house and all the details, and now my subconscious mind can start to work out the details. Eventually, I'll be sitting on the front porch in those dark brown wicker rocking chairs.

Create the vision of your home. You deserve to live in the one you love.

Your Career

This one is a doozy! Here's why: career is the basis of everything we do. It's where we make our money, and since money brings freedom, our career is really important.

Let's talk about yours. Do you like what you're doing now? Can you see yourself there for the long term? Is this career right for you?

If the answer is yes, then you can check off the box next to this item as complete.

If the answer is maybe—or even hell, no—then let's stop there and think.

We spend most of our day—and for some of us, our nights—at work. This takes us away from our family, our friends, and our lives. At the end of the day, if we aren't happy being there, and don't find any reward in our job, we are going to be unhappy. It's that simple.

Now, let's be real: work is *work*, not all fun and games.

You're not afraid of hard work—I already know that about you. I'm talking about a situation that isn't supporting who you are and the life you want to live. Even if you make a lot of money and don't like your job, you won't be happy. You know that money alone does not bring happiness.

Be honest with yourself and, if your current job isn't the right fit, decide to make a change. It may be that you're in the right career, but at the wrong company. Maybe your supervisor is difficult and does not appreciate you; maybe the commute is too long, affecting your ability to exercise and spend time with your family.

There are many reasons why your current company may not be working for you, and you already know if you need to send out your résumé.

Or it may be that you're in the wrong career. If so, start looking at other options.

If you have your own business, it may be time to sell it or close it down and start something new with your skill set. I'm not underestimating how huge this step would be, but staying in a role that isn't fulfilling just won't work.

Your well-being is at risk. If you're going to have a kick-ass life, you must find a career where you are valued and appreciated.

Start slow, and accept you're going to make a change. You might not take drastic action today or tomorrow, but you're going to begin looking at your options. Open your mind to the possibilities, thereby inviting possibilities into your life.

To really kick ass, you must be content with your career.

That doesn't mean you're going to love it every day, but it does mean knowing that you're where you belong. We all grow and change, and transitioning into a new career is normal. Maybe your current job was acceptable for many years, but now you have outgrown it.

Change is uncomfortable, but from time to time, we have to step out of our comfort zone into the unknown. Sometimes we stay in bad situations simply because they are familiar; we know it's bad, but at least we know what to expect. That just won't work for us anymore, because we aren't looking for "it's not good, but it's familiar."

Oh, no, that isn't even close to what we want and need. That, my friend, is called settling. Settling isn't going to allow us to kick ass and have an awesome life!

The people I have observed who are living their dream life, who are kicking ass at life, took a chance somewhere along the way (and maybe still are taking chances). Some of them started their own businesses. Some of them quit a long-term stable job to go to a small start-up company so they could work from home and have more personal time.

Taking a chance is part of the deal—no risk, no reward.

Simply making up your mind and deciding to make a change is half of the battle and a huge step in the right direction. Your subconscious mind will start to conjure up other opportunities, and you will be aware and open to them.

Start by deciding. Start today.

Your Spouse/Significant Other

Now we are going to look at our relationship with our spouse or significant other. This is the person whom we have chosen to share our life with on a day-to-day basis. That is quite a big decision.

When I got married the first time, I didn't think very much about the future with that person. I know that sounds strange, but I was more concerned about the present; I wanted to have a child, and my clock was ticking. The sound was getting louder and louder—*tick...tick...tick*—like a time bomb ready to explode. I was literally running out of time.

I got married based on that situation, without thinking about the life commitment I was making. That marriage gave me a child, and she's the best thing that has ever happened to me, but the marriage itself didn't stick. We were not life partners; we were temporary partners.

It's a good idea to be clear about the type of relationship you have. Is it a "let's have some fun and see how long it lasts" relationship, or "you're my soulmate and this is going to last forever"? Or maybe you don't know yet.

Find out as soon as possible so you can be clear with each other, not operate under false pretenses, and waste no time.

Now, this may seem obvious, but there are women out there who, like me, haven't really asked themselves this question (fun, commitment, or life partner?) with the intent of giving and receiving an honest answer.

Once we know what kind of relationship we are in, we can act accordingly.

Allowing someone to share your life is a huge leap of faith. In healthy relationships, both people support the other in chasing their dreams without judgment, insecurity, or fear. But a healthy relationship, as we all know, isn't so easy to find.

If you're in one, you're blessed and should hold this relationship close. Appreciate and nurture it with all that you have.

If you're in an unhealthy relationship, you already know that, *and* you know you deserve better. Maybe you're hanging onto it because you're not ready to let it go just yet; the sex is good but not much else in the relationship is fulfilling. Perhaps you simply don't want to be alone; maybe you're in love and know that you're going to be heartbroken, or you think they will change and become that person who you thought they were when you first met.

Bottom line: You cannot live a kick-ass life if you're in an unhealthy relationship. It's not possible. The two aren't compatible.

If you're working to become your best self—and you are, or you would not be reading this book—then all of your hard work and commitment won't work if your significant other isn't supporting you and is instead causing conflict. The relationship will hold you back and sabotage your overall happiness and ability to kick ass in life.

Consider how great an influence your spouse or significant other has over you—your behavior, your self-esteem, your mindset. It's obvious they affect your life. Therefore, you have to be careful who you let in. You're giving your time, energy, and yourself to this person, so make sure they are worth it.

If the relationship isn't adding to your life and you're not married, and don't have children, consider stepping away. Take time away from the relationship and see how you feel.

You might want to speak with a therapist to help work through your emotions and identify if it's time to end things. Letting go of an unhealthy relationship makes room for the person you're meant to be with—the person who will make you happy and fulfilled in your relationship.

If you're married and/or have children, it's not so easy to throw in the towel. I divorced my husband when my daughter was nine years old. It was the hardest thing I ever did. I was unhappy for so many years.

Living in the lost days as a workaholic in an unhappy marriage took a toll on me. I knew I had to make a change, but the idea of hurting my husband (he was living in denial and didn't want a divorce), and turning my daughter's life upside-down were devastating thoughts. And that was without considering the financial stress and unknowns.

It was easier to stay, and so I did, for many years after the relationship was over. I didn't have my toolboxes then, and I was not working on the marriage. I was hiding behind my work and wasting precious time.

That is the worst thing you can do.

Relationships are personal. It's easy to give advice and pass judgment, but only you know your situation. Others will tell you what they think you should do. Use the skills in your toolboxes to improve your life and your relationship. And don't isolate yourself; consider seeing a therapist for professional advice.

If you're single—or should I say, sassy and single—live it up! Single and kicking ass is quite a combination! When I was single, I always felt like I "needed" to meet someone, which is ridiculous. I wish I could go back in time and change my perception of singlehood.

Looking back, that was one of the best times of my entire life. I just didn't know it. I thought I was "missing something."

Single is a time in your life that is to be embraced. It's all about you! How great is that? You can focus all your attention on yourself, guilt-free. Take this time to celebrate you! Apply all the things that we have covered in this book and be the kind of person who any man or woman would love to meet.

Of course, being single can get lonely, and maybe you really want to be in a relationship. I get it. But here is the truth: There is no way to speed it up. It's about fate, about divine timing in the universe. You don't get to control it, no matter how organized you are at scheduling and planning, no matter how many dating sites you're on.

This is one of those things that you have to let go and let it be. When the time is right, the right person will come along, and you will both know it. Until then, enjoy your space and your life. Remain open to meeting new people, but don't force it.

After my divorce, I was looking for my soulmate and, in the process, have some fun.

After being in an unhealthy, no-sex relationship for many years, I was handed a get-out-of-jail-free card. I discovered my lost sexuality. I was having fun and rediscovering the person that I lost so many years ago.

Rejoice in being single. Single rocks!

Regardless of your relationship status, this is an area that you need to focus on and continue working on. It's too important to be ignored.

27
Rewards

You're a hard worker. You set goals. You take risks. You do whatever it takes to be the best version of yourself. You're reliable; if you say you're going to do something, you do it, and people know they can count on you. You're always learning new things to improve your life—that's why you're holding this book in your hands.

Now it's time to reward yourself. You deserve it and don't need to apologize for it.

Think about something you want. It can be anything. It doesn't have to be expensive; it might be a day off from work where your phone is off for an entire day, or a full treatment at the spa, or a new suit, or an amazing dress you've been coveting, or a purse that costs more than your car payment.

Whatever it is, find a way to buy it as a reward to yourself.

Yes, I know that sounds a little elaborate and we all know money doesn't grow on trees, but it does grow in your mindset. Here's the thing, though…if it's something you really want—not just a passing thought, but you really, *really* want it and have been thinking about it for a long time—you deserve it.

Now, if you don't have the money at present, start a savings account for whatever it is. Open an account and name the account for this item. Example—*Paula's Spa Day Savings Account.* Naming it will make it real.

If you're going to follow the guidelines for a balanced, healthy life, you're going to be working hard at life. None of the things in this book are easy. If they were easy, everyone would be doing them.

If you're kicking ass at life, you deserve to reward yourself.

If it's something big and extravagant that you have to save for, that's okay, because eventually you will get it. Maybe you can cut out your daily coffee run or make your lunch instead of eating out. Then you can add that money to your savings account. Any extra money that shows up in your budget can go into that account. Just opening the account and naming it will kick-start the process.

Other people may look at your life and think you spend too much on your car, house, and clothes. Their opinions are irrelevant and have no bearing on you, your world, or your happiness.

One of the bravest rewards I've ever given myself was a new Mercedes. At the time, I was making good money, but I didn't have a huge savings account, and I was a single mom, so some people believed that I needed to be careful with my money.

The problem was, I have never liked "being careful." Just the sound of those words carries a fearful tone. I have always believed that if you hold on tightly to money, it does not flow freely in your life. You need to spend it to make it and spend it to enjoy it; either way, you need to spend it. This doesn't mean you shouldn't save money for retirement and emergency situations; it simply means you deserve to spend some of the money on things that bring you joy.

When I purchased my Mercedes, I was driving a Lexus SUV. It was still in good shape and served a purpose, but it was a muted, conservative gray—it looked boring, and didn't represent me at all. This was after my divorce and during the "fun" phase, so a new car seemed like a good idea.

I had never had a red car, and always thought they were too flashy for me. I decided to visit a Mercedes dealership to look at a dark blue model that seemed like a good realtor car—not too flashy, but it still had some pizzazz.

I was standing in the parking lot at the dealership when one of the salespeople drove by in the model I liked, but it was bright cherry red. My head turned so quickly the salesperson must have thought I got whiplash.

I knew right then I would be buying a red Mercedes. I was nervous, not sure I could afford it, and it seemed so out of character.

But I changed my mindset and followed my heart and not too long after that, I was driving my new wheels with the sunroof down, music blasting, feeling more alive than I had in years.

Was it practical? No.

Was it a great investment? No.

It was a *reward*. And I never regretted it.

Rewarding yourself is a reminder that you're worth all your hard work.

28

No Time
Like the Present

Now that you have all this information, you're suited up and about to take on the world. You're ready to improve the areas of your life that have been holding you back from your full potential. You're ready, truly ready, to maximize your full potential. You're tired of dancing around the subjects that you know need to be addressed.

Quite simply—you're ready to kick ass and have a life.

The people in your world will sense a change, and more than that, they will witness it full on. *You* are going to change, and therefore you will behave differently.

In general, people don't like change, so be prepared and know not everyone will be supportive. For example, when you start implementing your Time Toolbox and spending time with your husband every day, and then implementing your Sex Toolbox, your marriage will start to shift and improve. You may stop complaining to your best friend about your spouse, and your friend may miss the old you.

Or when you implement your Exercise Toolbox, you will be eating healthy, and therefore your weekly pizza night with a longtime friend won't be as appealing to you.

As you make changes, the people closest to you will be forced to accept those changes, and some may grow distant or pull away. Some relationships may end. The new you may make people uncomfortable. They may even feel threatened, or insecure about their own life.

Go with the flow and stay on your track. Recognize this when it happens and know that is normal and part of the growth process.

There is no time like the present to start applying the eight toolboxes.

It's easy to procrastinate. If you catch yourself saying, "I will start tomorrow," change that thought to "I will start today." The sooner you begin, the sooner you will benefit from the positive changes in your life.

If you get off track, reset and start over.

The time for change is now.

Your kick-ass life is waiting!

29

If I'm Not a Workaholic, Then Who Am I?

As you move forward in your growth and recovery, you may feel out of sorts. Life as you know it will change drastically.

You will be taking care of yourself physically and emotionally for the first time in what may be an exceptionally long time. Your identity and very existence will be rocked; your entire routine changed.

Though these are positive changes, it will still be an adjustment. You will be learning who you are and remembering the person you lost when you became a workaholic.

The first year I began to apply the eight toolboxes into my life, I felt anxious all the time. When I would do something related to my personal life that was not benefiting my career, I felt guilty. It took months of applying the toolboxes to start to feel calm and centered.

I slowly felt better. I literally had to learn who I was as a person. What do I enjoy doing? What hobbies do I like? What is my favorite type of exercise? I spent so many years singularly focused on my career, I had no idea who I was or what I enjoyed.

Enjoy the process of self-discovery. It's part of the recovery.

It can be scary at first, but then it will start to be fun.

You're not your job; you're so much more than that. Your job and career are just one piece of what makes you who you are.

In the self-discovery phase, pay attention to the people, places, things you're drawn to. Even your fashion style may begin to change. When we are living as workaholics, we aren't focused on ourselves, and now that we have turned our eye toward our inner desires and self-care, things will look different.

A friend of mine was a workaholic for most of her life. My friend worked from home, so she wore her pajamas most of the morning, eventually changing into sweatpants and a T-shirt.

She spent her days, nights, and weekends in her office in front of the computer. She didn't wear makeup, and her hair was almost always pulled back in a ponytail. After the cracks in the foundation became larger, and her health deteriorated, she decided it was time to finally make a change. She applied the eight toolboxes to her life.

A year later, we met for lunch. I was seated at a table on the patio outside, enjoying the sunshine and waiting for my friend to arrive. When I glanced up, she was standing in front of me with a smile so big, it warmed my soul.

I was speechless!

She had a new hairstyle. Her long gray hair, now golden brown, framed her face in a flattering shoulder-length style. She had lost at least twenty-five pounds and was wearing a black skirt, light blue top, and sparkly sandals. I couldn't believe she was the same person.

We visited for two hours that day—both using our time from our Time Toolboxes. I asked her how her life had changed since becoming a recovering workaholic.

Her blue eyes sparkled. "At first it was hard, and I would slip back into my old ways, but after a couple of months I would revert back to my toolboxes and start over. Eventually I was able to apply the Time Toolbox consistently and those two hours became the highlight of my day. I realized how much I'd been neglected myself and my health. Just applying the Time Toolbox alone, I noticed a drastic difference in my state of mind.

"As I applied the other toolboxes, I started to feel like a different person. I looked in the mirror and didn't recognize my myself, I hadn't even realized my hair was completely gray! I knew I had some gray, but really had no idea. I was also in denial about my weight gain. Since I only wore sweatpants, it was easier to tell myself I had gained a few pounds and I would start eating better and exercising 'tomorrow.' Now, I feel like a brand-new version of myself, someone that I just met and that I really like.

Her smile and the spark in her eyes said it all.

Live and Let Live

Live your life on your terms, no one else's. Other people's opinions are irrelevant. Our truth is our own. We don't need people's approval to make it true.

When I applied my Time Toolbox, I realized how much time I was spending on things that don't matter. I didn't watch television, but always had my phone with me. I formed a habit of checking my social media accounts throughout the day—a quick, easily accessible distraction. The problem was, I was wasting my time on something that didn't bring me joy.

Social media gives the illusion that everyone has a wonderful life. It inundates us with pictures of smiling people, going amazing places, doing amazing things. When I look at these images, I feel as though I must be the most boring soul on the planet.

Why are we so interested in other people's lives but willing to ignore our own? It's a distraction from our own issues. Our issues will take work to fix, and we aren't ready to do that work, so we look for a quick and easy distraction. If it's not the phone, it's the television, where we spend hours staring at something we aren't really interested in.

I realized I was spending hours a day scrolling through social media admiring people's lives, and yet I couldn't find even one hour to spend with my husband, child, or best friend. When I started implementing my toolboxes, I became very aware of how my time was being allocated.

Once I became aware of my habits, I found myself scrolling on social media less and less. Stepping away from this activity was a quite an eye-opener; I had no idea how much time, energy, and effort I had been spending there.

It's far more productive to spend time applying the tools in your toolboxes. This doesn't mean you can't include social media in your life. It's an excellent way to stay in touch with family and friends, especially those who don't live near us—but don't let it dominate your time. And don't use it as a comparison tool.

Remember, social media is just a glimpse into other people's lives—the good parts, the parts they want people to see.

Other people will start to notice you're changing. Some will applaud you, and others will pull away, threatened by the new you.

Don't concern yourself with anybody else's opinion. We all have our own journey.

The more you practice living your new lifestyle, the more evolved your view on life will become. Your perception of yourself and the world has changed.

Be proud of the person you're becoming— you're kicking ass, and it shows!

Conclusion

If you have been applying the eight toolboxes and lessons from this book, your life has changed. You have improved the quality of your life and are rediscovering the things you like to do, spending time with your loved ones, and taking care of your emotional and physical self.

These are no small accomplishments!

Take a minute to look back at your journey and how far you have traveled.

Think about how you felt when you opened this book for the first time. Maybe you were searching for self-help books when this one caught your eye. You knew in that moment that you wanted and needed to make a change in your life, and you took a chance on this book.

You were willing to take the time to work on your life, to admit that you needed to make changes. It takes courage, strength, and effort to make those changes, so acknowledge that you're making progress and be proud of your accomplishments.

Think about the steps that you have taken to live a better life.

Be proud of each and every accomplishment that you have made.

As life moves forward, chances are things won't slow down, and our lives will never be perfectly Zen. Our professional and personal life will continue to evolve, and we will be busier than ever.

It's easy to fall back into our old ways, to skip our workout, to sneak back into our office when we should be asleep. Be aware of the temptation, and when those old habits resurface, apply your toolboxes one by one until they become a routine in your life again.

It's normal to have moments of difficulty and to slip. Life will throw curveballs that put you off track.

Be kind to yourself and restart again as soon as possible. As your life improves, you will realize how important it is to continue to apply the toolboxes regularly.

A few years ago, my mother became extremely ill. She was diagnosed with cancer and had to undergo several surgeries. I'm awfully close to my mom, so this threw my entire life into a tailspin. All the good habits I'd created disappeared overnight.

I was at the hospital day and night, my diet and exercise were off track, and I was not taking care of myself. Stress took over my life. I decided to allow myself the time I needed to be at the hospital and focus only on the Time Toolbox, the Exercise Toolbox, and the Sleep Toolbox.

During that difficult phase, my Time Toolbox was used every morning to meditate and pray. I started my day by allowing myself this time, and this one simple change made a huge difference in my state of mind.

I applied my Exercise Toolbox by exercising for thirty minutes in the morning before going to the hospital. By doing this, I was able to set the intention for the day to be healthy. This changed my eating habits at the hospital.

If I wouldn't have used this toolbox, I would have grabbed just anything for lunch and dinner, and my former unhealthy habits would have been activated. By taking care of myself, I was better equipped to be there for my mom. I was more centered and able to be stronger for her, myself, and my family.

It's so easy to fall into our old habits, especially under stress.

Apply the toolboxes during all the phases of your life, especially the most challenging ones. If you aren't able to apply all of them, select the most important ones.

Using just one toolbox will make a difference, but the more the merrier.

Life will always have up and downs. We are always going to have stressful moments. Remember they are just a phase.

One of my favorite quotes is "this too shall pass"

Knowing this, and reminding yourself of it often, will help to keep the stress under control.

Be reminded that stressful times are just a phase—they won't last forever.

Live in the Now

I have always liked the song, "Cats in the Cradle" by Harry Chapin. When I was younger, I liked the sound of it; it has a melody that makes you feel something, as if you know something meaningful is being said just by the tone of the lyrics.

Now that I'm older, I know the meaning of the song all too well.

In case you don't know it, it's about a father who is too busy to schedule time to be with his newborn son. As life evolves, the father decides he wants to spend time with his son, but now the son is grown and has his own interests. As life evolves further, the son becomes an adult and now he's just like his father, too busy to make time.

This song presents the classic case of thinking we have time to do the things we want to do "later."

We all think that we can put things off until tomorrow, somehow believing that time will wait for us.

Looking back, I would give anything to have a second chance to spend quality time with my daughter, to be present with her and enjoy those early years, to enjoy the vacations that we took together, to read her a bed time story, to go to the school play and so much more.

It's my loss.

We only get one shot at getting it right—yet we lie to ourselves and pretend we have time to do everything we want to do "later."

How can we say we will do it later when we don't even know if we have tomorrow?

Let's face it, none of us know how much time we have on this earth, so let's stop lying to ourselves. "Later," my friend, may never come.

If it's important to you, do it now.

The moment you have is to be seized! Do what is important to you. Take care of yourself and apply the eight toolboxes.

When you live a healthy, balanced life, you are at your best and can give your best to those you love. When you're depleted, tired, and not taking care of yourself, you have nothing to give.

Life moves quickly, regardless of our circumstances. There is never a good time to get sick or lose a loved one. Life will keep moving at record speed, even when you desperately need it to slow down.

Time doesn't wait for anyone.

Now we know there is no time to waste, we can't work our lives away with the plan that we can take that trip *later*, make time for that person *later*, buy that house *later*, or exercise and take care of our health *later*.

Later doesn't exist, all we have is *now*.

Yesterday is gone. The things we did or didn't do are in the past. Leave them there.

Be the best version of yourself today, in this moment.

Now.

Embrace Success

As you become more and more successful in your life, be proud of yourself and your accomplishments.

It's easy to downplay your greatness. Sometimes it's easier to downplay how smart you are in order to allow others to feel better. This move does not serve you, no way—you're way too smart for that!

That doesn't mean you have to brag about your accomplishments, but just be proud of everything you have worked so hard for. Continue to grow. Be true to yourself.

There are people who will be threatened by your success. It will make them uncomfortable because it magnifies their own insecurities. If there are people like this in your life, it's important for you to accept that is their issue, not yours.

If you're smarter or more capable than your supervisor—and everyone knows it—this may cause your supervisor to lash out at you or try to make you look bad in front of others. Don't lower your standards to make them feel better or more secure.

This difficulty comes with success. It's part of the deal.

Do your best to surround yourself with confident people who are your cheerleaders in life. They want you to succeed. The others will have to deal with their own insecurities.

Success is yours because you have worked your ass off for it—so embrace it!

KICK ASS!

You need to make sure that, at the end of your life, you don't have any regrets.

If you can honestly say you live your life every day in the now, fully present for your loved ones and yourself, that you make time for the things that matter to you, then you can say that you're living, not just surviving.

You're a bright, shining star with endless potential.

You have learned so much about yourself, and you're willing to do the work that is required to have a kick-ass life.

Your career is only one part of who you are—in fact, it's only a sliver of who you are. You're no longer giving your entire life for your career because you know there is so much more to experience and enjoy during your time on earth.

You will continue to grow and prosper.

The past is just that—the past.

Focus on your future.

It's bright, just like you!

Until We Meet Again

Thank you for sharing your time and part of your journey with me. I hope this book has a positive impact on your life.

If you started reading it as a workaholic, my wish and prayer for you is that you have implemented the eight tool-boxes, and many other positive habits that we discussed, and the habits you're creating are transforming your life into the one you desire and so richly deserve!

I hope you're taking time for yourself to exercise and eat well, enjoying your hobbies, spending time with your spouse or significant other, having great sex, and experiencing wealth and freedom in ways you never knew possible.

I hope you're allowing money to flow freely in your life while taking time off to vacation and be present with the people you love.

Life is short.

We hear this all the time, but most people don't actually do anything to change the course of their life. They just watch it pass by or work it away.

Sharing my story with you was emotional, and—at times—embarrassing. I was not at my best for many years. I'm not proud of the lost days, but I hope by sharing my story, your life will change for the better, and you will learn from my mistakes.

The workaholic lifestyle I lived is very far removed from my current one. It's hard for me to comprehend I actually wasted all of those years. I wasn't there for my family, friends, or myself, but as you have learned in this book, it's unproductive to dwell on the mistakes of the past.

The most important and powerful thing we can do is live in the now and create the life we want and we deserve—the life that is available to all of us for the taking.

Enjoy, live, laugh, and never stop believing in yourself. And until we meet again…

Kick Ass and Have a Life!

TOOLBOXES RECAP
Time

Two hours per day

Who do I want to spend time with?

_____

How do I want to use my two hours?

_____

How am I being called to use my two hours?

_____

_____

Notes

_____

_____

_____

_____

_____

_____

_____

Sex/Intimacy

Two hours two times per week

Who do I want to reserve time for in my sex toolbox?

_____

_____

What can I do to be more intimate with my partner?

_____

_____

_____

_____

Twenty Years

Visualize and Create Your Future

One hour once per month

What memories do I want to create for my future?

_____

_____

_____

_____

What can I do now to create memories that I will treasure in my Twenty years toolbox?

_____

_____

_____

_____

_____

Notes

_____

_____

_____

_____

_____

_____

_____

_____

_____

_____

_____

_____

_____

Exercise

Thirty minutes every day

What type of exercise am I committed to?

_____

_____

What day and time will I exercise?

_____

_____

What are my exercise goals?

_____

_____

Notes

_____

_____

_____

_____

_____

_____

Sleep

Review your sleep routine every day (fifteen minutes)

What changes can I make to sleep better?

_____

_____

_____

What are my sleep goals? Review the sleep toolbox.

_____

_____

_____

Notes

_____

_____

_____

_____

_____

_____

_____

_____

Vacation

Plan your vacation

Vacation fourteen days per year

Where do I want to go on vacation? (dream big!)

_____

_____

_____

Who will cover for me at work?

_____

_____

_____

Notes

_____

_____

_____

_____

_____

_____

_____

Hobby

Two hours one time per week

What are my favorite hobbies?

_____

_____

_____

What do I enjoy that could become a new hobby?

_____

_____

_____

_____

Notes

_____

_____

_____

_____

_____

_____

_____

Friends

Reach out one time per week

Spend time together once per month (two hours)

Which friend(s) do I want to connect with?

_____

_____

_____

_____

What activity do I want to schedule with this person?

_____

_____

_____

_____

Notes

_____

_____

_____

_____

_____

References

J.R.R. TOLKIEN *"All we have to decide is what to do with the time that is given us."* https://www.goodreads.com/author/quotes/656983.J_R_R_Tolkien

"This too shall pass." The original origin for this quote was unable to be verified.

The Five Love Languages. Gary Chapman. https://www.goodreads.com/book/show/23878688-the-5-love-languages

Every Picture Tells a Story, Studio album by Rod Stewart

"Cat's in the Cradle," song by Harry Chapin

Author's Note

Thank you for taking the time to read **Kick Ass and Have a Life.** When I started writing my story, I realized that to share it with you; I would have to expose the parts of my life that I am not proud of; we all have an image that we project to the world, the image of me in the lost days is not an image I am proud of. Still, if my story sheds light on the dysfunction of the workaholic lifestyle and can assist in recovery, then it is worth sharing.

As you implement each of the eight toolboxes into your daily life, I hope you are experiencing the positive changes that come from being fully present in your life. I also hope you are experiencing more joy than you ever imagined.

I'd love to hear about how you're doing and how you're progressing.

Please visit my social media pages and website to keep in touch. I am looking forward to connecting in the future.

Blessings,

Paula Marie

www.KickAssAndHaveALife.com

PaulaMarieBooks/

PaulaMarieBooks

Books_Paula

PaulaMarieBooks/